NEW GENERATION PO

This special issue of *Poetry Review* is a
to the 20 books selected for the promotion. It features each
poet in depth, reviewing their work so far and including,
where possible, **new work** that will appear in their
next collections. In many cases, the poets also contribute articles and reviews
that display their own interests.

Highlights include Glyn Maxwell visiting the Trinidad **Carnival**
recently to meet his old friend and tutor, the Nobel Prize-winning poet, Derek
Walcott, and Simon Armitage on his recent **American** reading tour. The
New Generation is examined from many facets, including the reactions of
politicians like Roy Hattersley,
Kenneth Baker, Denis Healey and Neil
Kinnock, and **schoolchildren** to a
poem from each of the 20 books. Seven of
the 20 poets are **Scottish** – Douglas Dunn
celebrates a new era for Scottish poetry. Don
Paterson contributes a hilarious **diary** of
the New Gen launch, and Gavin Ewart finds
in the **tabloids** and rugby songs techniques
reminiscent of Medieval verse. Continuing the
Poetry Society's **Poets on Poets** theme,
we have David Dabydeen on the Gawain Poet,
Lavinia Greenlaw on Akhmatova, Pauline
Stainer on David Jones, Michael Donaghy on
John Updike. And John Hegley is **profiled.**

Very many people have helped to make the
New Generation possible. The following
provided funding:
The Arts Council
The David Cohen Family Charitable Trust
The Esmée Fairbairn Charitable Trust
The Foundation for Sport and the Arts
The British Council
Waterstone's Booksellers
Anvil Press Poetry
Bloodaxe Books
Jonathan Cape
Chatto & Windus
Faber & Faber
Oxford University Press
Secker & Warburg
Lord Goodman
Poetry Review is especially grateful to the
Foundation for Sport and the Arts for making
this expanded issue possible, and to the British
Council for buying copies for distribution
overseas.
Please see 'How We Made New Gen' (page 52)
for further information

POETRY
REVIEW

Spring 1994
Volume 84
Number 1

EDITOR
PETER **F**ORBES

ASSISTANT EDITOR
KEVAN **J**OHNSON

Society needs Poetry: JOIN *the* Poetry Society

If you write, read, teach or promote poetry, join the Society to develop your knowledge and enjoyment of Britain's most buoyant and participatory artform.

You Will Receive ...

POETRY NEWS. Our new look quarterly newsletter packed with opportunities, ideas and comment. Special issues and supplements will focus on poetry and education, libraries, festivals and new writers.

POETRY REVIEW, Britain's leading poetry magazine: 'essential reading for anyone who wants to keep up to date with new poetry. It's the magazine which readers of poetry can't do without.' **– Douglas Dunn, Whitbread Prize Winner**

Discounts On ...

THE NATIONAL POETRY COMPETITION. This is open to all – with thirteen cash prizes totalling £5,250 – and has built up a remarkable track record for discovering new talent and affirming the reputations of established names. Past prizewinners include Tony Harrison, Carol Ann Duffy, and Jo Shapcott. Last year's winner, Sam Gardner, was a newcomer to poetry, unknown – until he won £3,000 and saw his poem published by the *Guardian*.

THE SCRIPT, a unique service to all those who write poetry. Fill out a questionnaire specially devised to help you think about how and why you write, then send it in with a sample of your poetry for a 'diagnosis' from a skilled professional poet and a 'prescription' of new ideas and further reading.

POETRY READINGS, talks and events around the UK.

INFORMATION & IMAGINATION SEMINARS: seminars, fact sheets, training courses for teachers, librarians, promoters, poets and all those who love poetry.

HELPING POETRY THRIVE IN BRITAIN TODAY

NEW GENERATION POETS
POETRY REVIEW SPRING 1994 (Vol 84 No 1)

Talking About the New Generation

Peter Forbes on the new, the old, and 'the last gasp of a system of patronage'

At first sight, the list of twenty New Generation poets is perhaps narrower than it might have been. Judged as personalities and readily tagged types, they don't entirely live up to the journalistic clichés of the new pluralism, regionalism, and the rise of the working class voice. There are no performance poets, no Afro-Caribbean poets (the one Caribbean, David Dabydeen is of Indian descent). There is a healthy and notable contingent of Scots (seven) and a respectable if not startling number of women (eight). But the moment you examine these twenty books, the distinctiveness and stubborn, even wilful individuality of these poets emerges like some Japanese paper flower unscrolling in water.

This true plurality makes any group portrait a risky venture – it totally defeated the editors of *The New Poetry*, for example – but there are patterns, which we hope our coverage will elucidate, and there are reasons for the apartness of many of these poets.

Eliot famously said of William Blake that he worked within no tradition, and felt he had to invent a religion and world view as well as to write original poetry. Eliot disapproved, believing that innovation should be confined to the poetry, that it was best written within a – for him – Christian, Royalist, Conservative framework (he accepted that for others this might read: Atheist, Republican and Communist but there had to be *something*). Most of the New Generation poets have followed Blake, rather than Eliot. It is not hard to see why. In England especially, the '80s was a time of social atomization – after all, it was official government policy. The centre could not hold in anything. Private worlds, subcults, proliferated. The central channels of literary culture, the BBC, Oxbridge, Penguin books, Faber & Faber, the *New Statesman* and *Listener*, all had to adapt to being just one player amongst several. One of these has already foundered and others may follow. It became less likely that any two people would have seen the same TV programme, read the same book, or share any culture at all in a meaningful sense.

Ten years ago, new poets had strong links both

> One would expect a new generation to be angry young turks, spitting fire at their immediate predecessors, the fat cats with all the controlling jobs, but for most of this century there has been deep collusion between the established generation and the newcomers.

with each other and with a tradition, as had always been the case in England. Craig Raine, Andrew Motion, James Fenton, Blake Morrison, and Christopher Reid, for all their differences, had a programme – basically, the Movement plus visual fireworks – and eagerly set about promulgating it by editing magazines, reviewing strenuously, editing anthologies, and running the major publishers' poetry lists. Such coteries do exist among the New Generation, but as a loose network dispersed about the regions, with a modest infrastructure of magazines and publishers. Only the Scots have the full-blown proselytizing tendency, and, interestingly, Crawford and Herbert, the twin pillars of the new Scottish poetry industry, learnt their trade at Oxford University, the traditional forcing ground for ambitious poetry promoters.

There are regional centres with similar ambitions in Yorkshire (Kennedy and Morley editing *The New Poetry*, the activities centered on the Poetry Business in Huddersfield) and Hull, centered on the magazine *Bête Noire*, but most of the English poets in the New Generation do not edit or review, or do anything much beyond write their poems and earn a living. Simon Armitage, who came up through the Huddersfield hothouse, seems to have had editing (for the *Guardian* and Chatto) thrust upon him by his fame. He had no editing and little reviewing experience before starting these jobs. In any case, in England the activists are not New Generation poets: John Osborne of *Bête Noire* was a judge for the promotion, not a poet in it; David Kennedy and David Morley are poet-editors who are still making their way as poets.

We sent questionnaires to all the poets to try to flush out affiliations both to contemporary poets and to tradition. The only unifying feature of their responses was their relative disdain for English poetry of the 20th century and their enthusiasm for American and European poetry. Every poet who returned a questionnaire cited at least one American poet, and the runaway winner was Elizabeth Bishop with five mentions: from poets as different as Jamie McKendrick, Sarah Maguire, Kathleen Jamie, Don

Paterson, and Lavinia Greenlaw. This is something of a phenomenon and suggests perhaps a future *Poetry Review* symposium. Perhaps Bishop is a poet who in sanctioning finding your own way – becoming a curious traveller in your own and other countries – has served as an inspiration to poets without a central tradition? Robert Lowell received three mentions and many poets received two: Auden, Graves, MacDiarmid, Heaney, Frost, Berryman, Edwin Morgan, Geoffrey Hill, Rilke. Another section of the questionnaire, asking for positive or negative responses to various mainstream movements and anthologies was widely disliked, but, re the 'thirties, MacNeice received several favourable comments, which made up for the general blank drawn by the compiler on this one.

European integrationists who despair of progress towards any kind of European sensibility (remember Gorbachev's 'our common European home') can take some heart from the New Generation (as can advocates of the Special relationship with America). Poets like Michael Hofmann, John Burnside, Susan Wicks, Jamie McKendrick, Elizabeth Garrett, Carol Ann Duffy, Lavinia Greenlaw do have European poetry (French, Spanish, German, Russian, Italian) in their bones. It is slightly surprising that East European influences were not cited, although we know they are there.

Isolation and intensity are the hallmarks of many these poets (although there is a group revolving around Paterson and Donaghy and their musical exploits, and no doubt the New Generation promotion itself will change poetic history by forging new relationships within the twenty). Pauline Stainer has peopled a world with painters and musicians, a glittering, brilliant and sometimes precious world, which despite its uncompromising nature can communicate readily – witness the responses to her poetry by children (see page 96) and politicians (see page 38) included in this issue. John Burnside works with computers but writes in the French mode about 'trees, sky, water'. Elizabeth Garrett has been compared to Emily Dickinson and E. J. Scovell and admits Donne as her prime influence, along with Graves in the 20th century. Ian Duhig may have affinities with other post-Muldoonian playful postmodernists, but his delightfully amused and amusing plundering of cultural and political movements and his Zen-like lurches of focus are entirely his own. Michael Hofmann is the most Lowellian but

> **Ian Hamilton's Oxford Companion to 20th Century Poetry ... compiled on the chain-letter principle of editing – one reliable chap recommending another – it represents a map of a lost empire, that famous hegemony.**

adds a strong European note and considerable personal idiosyncrasy. Glyn Maxwell's writing and career have been unlike anyone else's in recent times, culminating in his 'Shakespeare of the Suburbs' ploy of mounting productions of verse-plays in the garden of his parents' Welwyn home. One could go on. Susan Wicks, a late starter, acknowledging fiction and French literature as an influence, has no obvious connection with anyone else. Moniza Alvi has been part of the London scene for several years but her two main influences are her Pakistani origins and her work as a teacher. Simon Armitage, the best known of the younger poets, has cannily fused elements of his northern background with a thorough knowledge of American poetry, especially Lowell and Weldon Kees.

These poets are the true fruits of postmodernism: all cultures are now available to add to own's own inheritance, and there is no predicting what will appeal to a gifted poet growing up in Huddersfield, or Tunbridge Wells, for that matter. It is worth remembering that in 1982 Andrew Motion and Blake Morrison claimed 'a postmodernist wit –and nerve' for *their* poets in *The Penguin Book of Contemporary British Poetry*. Insofar as this was anything other than an attempt to add a little theoretical relevance to their choices, it seemed to refer merely to shifting visual frames of reference, as in the visual puns of Martian poetry ('the dustbins bulge like vol-au-vents)'. Paul Muldoon's postmodernism, though, is an exception, and he is something of a father figure to some of the New Generation, although only cited in one questionnaire response. In some of the New Generation poets (as in Muldoon) – Duhig (above all), Herbert, Maxwell, Paterson, Armitage, Crawford, Hofmann, Greenlaw – whole slabs of historical and cultural reference jostle, butt up against, and slip over each other in a form of linguistic plate tectonics.

Of all the poets here, the only 'traditional' poet in the sense of fully belonging to the Oxonian tradition, is Mick Imlah. He read English at Magdalen and John Fuller and James Fenton were his mentors. He was thus in a direct line to Auden, the central figure of English 20th century poetry, and an influence on several of the New Gens. But whereas Fenton and his Oxford friends dominated the early 'eighties, Imlah, at present, is a marginal figure who has only produced one book and that six years ago. (Compare the hectic productivity of Armitage and Maxwell).

There has been much loose talk about 'the ending of the Oxbridge hegemony' (there are seven New Generation poets who attended Oxford or Cambridge as under- or post-graduates – five Oxford and two Cambridge, and why does Oxford always win this race?). What is certain is that the New Generation Poets have broken a pattern that had become debilitating. One would *expect* a new generation to be angry young turks spitting fire at their immediate predecessors, the fat cats with all the controlling jobs, but for most of this century there has been a deep collusion between the established generation and the newcomers. There is a clear line from the Movement, through Ian Hamilton's Neo-Movement of the '70s to Blake Morrison, Andrew Motion and Craig Raine in the '80s. The benefits of this system – to everyone but the reader – are obvious. The older generation protect their declining years by having their nominees holding the key jobs, and the younger blossom under the benign gaze of the oldies. Of course there have always been mavericks like Ted Hughes and Tony Harrison who have refused to play the game but have nevertheless won universal acceptance through sheer force of talent and integrity, but the general principle holds.

The last gasp of this system of patronage is to be seen in Ian Hamilton's *Oxford Companion to 20th Century Poetry*, than which a less timely publication could scarcely be imagined – rather like running a tea-planter's convention in 1947 India. Compiled on the chain-letter principle of editing – one reliable chap recommending another and to hell with the inevitable gaps – it represents a map of a lost empire, that famous hegemony. Exactly half of the New Generation Poets are excluded (although W. N. Herbert is dealt with by a patronizing cross-reference to 'Lallans'), but anyone who is part of Ian Hamilton's extended family of Oxbridge D. Phil.'s and *TLS* contributors is in (the *TLS* Deputy Editor's entry is 50 per cent longer than Carol Ann Duffy's, presumably because Alan Jenkins is 'in the process of discovering his potential', whereas Duffy has merely won all the prizes going and is, in the words of one critic, on the way to becoming 'the representative poet of our times'). One reason for the exclusions is the book's instant obsolescence, many entries having been written nearly five years ago and never updated. (To declare an interest, *Poetry Review*, it is reassuring to read, 'has once more become more conventionally welcoming though much less comatose than its earlier self'.)

If the New Generation lies athwart the old Establishment, neither does it sit easily with older alternative powerbases. The promotion has elicited predictable rumblings from the Neo-Leavisites in Manchester, who now style themselves, on the masthead of *PN Review* as 'The Poetry Centre, Department of English'. At an Oxford Conference in February on 'The Poetry Industry' Nicholas Tredell brought a fierce indignation to bear on such iniquities as the citing of awards on the back of slim volumes and indeed, poetry prizes at all (he was, much of the time, ventriloquizing for Donald Davie and Michael Schmidt). At one point he held up Carol Ann Duffy's *Mean Time* – a rather drab-looking book of decidedly old-fashioned design, that belies its luminous contents – as a pernicious example of the effects of 'marketing'. In *PN Review 96* Michael Schmidt again attacks the marketing of the New Generation, quoting articles from the *Independent* as if they were the voice of the promotion itself. Unfortunately, we cannot control what the media say (see Don Paterson's account of the New Generation launch on page 58).

Only one key institution has played a significant role in the rise of the New Generation (besides this magazine, of course): Bloodaxe Books. Without such an independent, energetic, and hospitable publisher, prepared to back such disparate talents as Armitage, Maxwell, Jamie, Duhig, Stainer, Garrett and Herbert (amongst many more who almost made the twenty), these multiple fruits may well have withered on the vine. And Faber would not now be publishing Armitage, Paterson, and Wicks.

The individual poet who broke with the old tradition and established poetic independence as a viable option was Carol Ann Duffy. From the start she has always gone her own way, remaining loyal to small presses – Turret Books for pamphlets, Anvil for her full collections. Her style seemed to spring from no obvious poetic source, combining a brilliant ear for street voices, a natural lyricism, and a penchant for monologue. (Compare Duffy's monologues with Mick Imlah's 'The Zoologist's Bath' – Imlah is richly Browningesque and the essence of dusty Oxonianism; Duffy's have the stink of some new beast entering the language for the first time.) Although Carol Ann Duffy has spawned many disciples and you can see echoes of her bravado and one-word sentences in poets like Jackie Kay, Eva Salzman and Deryn Rees-Jones, her main influence has been the creation of space in which poets can be themselves.

Working with the poets over the last six months and reading and re-reading their books, my admiration for them has grown. They offer twenty distinct worlds, and as coherent and composed a response to our times as you'll find in any other artform. I commend them to you.

WATERSTONE'S
BOOKSELLERS

Waterstone's, Britain's finest nationwide stockists of poetry books, are proud to be sponsors of the New Generation Poets.

See and hear the following New Generation Poets reading at Waterstone's branches

Tuesday 3rd May, 7pm
John Burnside, Ian Duhig, Michael Hofmann, Jamie McKendrick
Waterstone's, 91 Deansgate, Manchester
Tel. 061 832 1992

Thursday 5th May, 7pm
Simon Armitage, Elizabeth Garrett, Pauline Stainer
Waterstone's, 36/38 Albion Street, Leeds
Tel. 0532 420839

Thursday 12th May, 7pm
Lavinia Greenlaw, Michael Hofmann, Glyn Maxwell
Waterstone's, 36/38 Albion Street, Leeds
Tel. 0532 420839

Tuesday 17th May, 7.30pm
Simon Armitage, Glyn Maxwell, Don Paterson
Waterstone's, 121 Charing Cross Road, London
Tel. 071 434 4291.

Wednesday 18th May, 7pm
WN Herbert
Waterstone's, 35 Commercial Street, Dundee
Tel. 0382 200322.

Thursday 19th May, 7pm
Simon Armitage, Ian Duhig
Waterstone's, 28-29 High Ousegate, York
Tel. 0904 628740.

Tuesday 24 May, 7pm
Robert Crawford, WN Herbert, Kathleen Jamie, Don Paterson
Waterstone's, 35 Commercial Street, Dundee
Tel. 0382 200322.

We have over 90 branches throughout the UK and Ireland.
For a full list *Tel. 081 742 3800*
Mail order *Tel. 0225 448 595*

SIMON ARMITAGE
Kid

SIMON ARMITAGE WAS BORN IN 1963 IN HUDDERSFIELD AND NOW LIVES IN NEARBY MARSDEN. HE read Geography at Portsmouth Polytechnic and now works as a probation officer in Manchester and also as Poetry Editor for Chatto & Windus. He won an Eric Gregory Award in 1988, and was one of four poets on the Poetry Society's *Catch Words* Tour in 1990. His first book, *Zoom* (Bloodaxe, 1989) was a Poetry Book Society Choice. *Kid* (Faber, 1992) won a Forward Prize. His latest collection is *Book of Matches* (Faber, 1993).

Brashness was the first note struck by Armitage: the first page of his first book has a poem called 'Snow Joke'. But his boisterous knack of turning pub talk into poetry ('if you only pay peanuts you're working with monkeys') tended to obscure his subtly insidious rhythms and lyrical ambitions. His Huddersfield colleague Peter Sansom said: 'He has found his voice early' and the voice, which is what draws people to Armitage, is an amalgam of an immaculate timing that enables him to pace a whole verse paragraph and not just the odd line or two, and a kind of toughly tender stance seen at its best in poems like 'Lines to a Long Lost Lover' in *Book of Matches*.

Armitage is fascinated by the American poet Weldon Kees who disappeared, a presumed suicide, by the Golden Gate Bridge in 1955, and he has borrowed Kees's persona Robinson – a man who stepped out of an Edward Hopper painting – for many of his poems. In both Kees and Armitage, Robinson is trailed – as though by a private detective – through lovingly detailed scenes of acute individual isolation and existential torment The attraction of this for a man who now has several real-life personæ is obvious – Armitage in conclave with a young offender, Armitage driving home over the Millstone Grit, Armitage sifting manuscripts at Chatto.

Like Glyn Maxwell, Armitage has been likened to Auden for his versatility, confidence and originality. Although some critics felt that *Book of Matches* saw him marking time, Armitage's work is exciting enough to ensure that his every appearance is eagerly awaited. **(PF)**

Simon Armitage writes:
Poetry's a big thing – there's more than one of it, so in making any kind of statement I'm only saying something personal rather than trying to be universal or prescriptive. For me, poetry has become a private thing, a dialogue between one part of myself and another. One informs and the other translates. It has also become part of my outlook or attitude, a core construct, and more and more I find myself wondering how much of the everyday world will make itself available for the purpose of poetry. But at the same time, through wanting to publish poetry, put it on general release and make it public property, the process of writing is always consciously overseen or overheard. It's conspiratorial, but by defi-

nition it will always lead to the gallows or the stocks. It's bugged, and the person listening in is once again the author. Writing has become a way of taking part without having to participate, and a way of being alone without being lonely or broken hearted.

More than that, in terms of *why* I write and why I write *what* I write, I suppose I believe that words have no meaning unless they're spoken, seen or heard, and that language can be a good thing, and the more good things that are spoken, seen or heard, the better.

Three influential 20th C. books:
W. H. Auden, *Collected Poems*; Ted Hughes, *Selected Poems* 1957-1981; Robert Lowell, *Life Studies*.

THREE POEMS BY SIMON ARMITAGE

Dream Holiday

On the first night, a yawn,
the noiseless opening and closing of a downstairs door.
The dog lifted an ear,
and the next day the dog was kennelled in the car.

On the next night, a sneeze or cough
was shredded paper or a flash gun going off.
The dog tapped its tail
and the next night the dog was taken out and docked.

On the third night, footsteps in the roof-space
were bars of gold loaded into a suitcase.
The dog yelped,
and there and then the dog was muzzled with a belt.

On the fourth night, the milky way
was the gang of sparks from a nylon stocking lifted
from a face; water in the cistern
whispered, the dog whimpered,

toenails clipped were cables snipped, cracked knuckles
were connections uncoupled, splintered wood
and fractured glass, the dog shat,
and for that the dog was taken out and shot.

On the last night we were cleaned out,
the sound of tearing metal – hinges, locks –
drowned by the thought
of a dog asleep like a stone in its box.

Before You Cut Loose

                                        put dogs on the list
of difficult things to lose. Those dogs ditched
on the North York Moors or the Sussex Downs

or hurled like bags of sand from rented cars
have followed their noses to market towns
and bounced like balls into their owners' arms.
I heard one story of a dog that swam
to the English coast from the Isle of Man,
and a dog that carried eggs and bacon
and a morning paper from the village
surfaced umpteen leagues and two years later,
bacon eaten but the eggs unbroken,
newsprint dry as tinder, to the letter.
A dog might wander the width of the map
to bury its head in its owner's lap,
crawl the last mile to dab a bleeding paw
against its own front door. To die at home,
a dog might walk its four legs to the bone.
You can take off the tag and the collar
but a dog wears one coat and one colour.
A dog got rid of – that's a dog for life.
No dog howls like a dog kicked out at night.
Try looking a dog like that in the eye.

Stray

So you had to dine
year in year out on a rusty chain
or salty washing line,

then chewed right through that makeshift tether
and one night strayed, still noosed
in a bitten-off length of leash and collar, sporting

a body that gnawed itself clear of the gallows,
burn marks, lesions to the skin,
that sort of thing.

Well, beginning tomorrow
you can feed for free at the butcher's bin
on sickening meat and poisonous marrow,

and take like a tramp
to the life of the street – go on,
get out – in bare feet.

Armitage in America

Auden wrote of his reading tours of the USA: 'God bless the U.S.A., so large, so friendly and so rich'.
Simon Armitage, *who toured for 10 days at the end of February, gives a '90s update*

On Wednesday the ninth he travelled east in a taxi at dawn, wearing a hat that would have been snowballed from his head had he worn it in his home town. Nine hours later, following numerous unscheduled stops and several rehearsals of the brace position he stumbled onto the tarmac in Washington D.C., from where he was conveyed by stretch limousine to The Double Tree Inn at the Colonnade, Baltimore, and slept like a corpse despite the activities of a visiting basketball team, practising their setpieces in the adjoining suite.

On Thursday the tenth, with the clock in his head now synchronized and the compass of his heart pointing in a new direction, he was transported to Loyola College through an avenue of trees crystallized with ice and seasoned with snow, and was met by professors McGuiness and McGuiness who heaped hospitality upon him, and toured him around the campus as if it were a property he might be interested in acquiring. A seminar on the situation of British Poetry passed off remarkably well, and he spoke thoughtfully and confidently as to the activities of some of his contemporaries and colleagues. Movements were explained, personalities were excused. Towards the last quarter of the second hour, and regarding his understanding of the American predicament, he was politely suspicious of the system of poetic auditions on the casting couches of academic institutions. On the subject of the L=A=N=G=U=A=G=E poets he very nearly overstepped the mark, but recovered ground with some memorable one-liners, and redeemed himself entirely by chattering endlessly and effortlessly on the subjects of prosody and cadence. There followed that very evening a reading of his own work, and for thirty-five minutes and eleven seconds he let fly his angular syllables till the great hall was an aviary of imported vowels and exotic consonants. Modesty would not allow him an encore, but he did rise from his seat on a second occasion to acknowledge the ongoing applause, and was happy to adorn copies of books with an extravagant and swashbuckling signature. For those moved to the point of purchase, further copies were available at the generously converted price of nine dollars and ninety-nine cents only.

Friday the eleventh was a morning of mild self-congratulation, and amusing himself with the notion that poetry might replace stand-up comedy as the next rock 'n roll, he took up his pen and a complimentary leaf of headed hotel notepaper to embark on a piece entitled 'I Say I Say I Say'. Later, in the bath tub, he discovered himself to be the victim of trench foot or some similar disorder – a surprise, he felt, considering the amount of time spent on his arse of late compared with the upright position, when expressed as a ratio. He shuddered at the thought of losing one or more of his lower digits – how vulnerable this might leave him in a world of thin ice where sure footing and perfect balance were everything. Nevertheless, this did not prevent him dragooning half the faculty to Hammerjack's nightclub that same evening to see Juliana Hatfield, the first lady of American pop. Slam dancing in the mosh pit was *de rigueur*, as was the workman-like intake of domestic bottled beer, leaving the end of the night, the small hours of the following morning and indeed the subsequent day open to speculation and invention.

Saturday the twelfth: no record of his movements.

On Sunday the thirteenth he learned that along with Babe Ruth, Baltimore also laid claim to Mr Edgar Allan Poe, and that the place of his death could be located in a part of town where the expiration of human life was a common occurrence, though rarely by natural causes. He also recalled that the same city was the birthplace of Mr O'Hara, and was pleased to saunter through its streets that afternoon, having been something of a Frank O'phile from an early age.

On Monday the fourteenth he fell from the sleep of a Randall Jarrell poem into umpteen uninterrupted miles of slums and shunting yards, Cleveland's twilight zone. Alighting from the overland rapid transit system he was spirited away in a private vehicle to a safe-house in the east of town, where he steamed for hours in a shallow bath, emerging perfumed and poached rather than pickled and over-easy. Sleep came quickly, as did the dawn.

On Tuesday the fifteenth he strode purposefully into Cleveland State University's Creative Writing Class, where he was generous with his praise and gracious with his criticism, even towards those poems which appeared as iron filings tipped across plain white paper without the organising presence of a magnet, and also to several pieces of xerography. Etch-A-Sketch, he thought. Spirograph. At the reading that night in an inverted pyramid masquerading as an amphitheatre he recited upwardly and outwardly, but even his most expressive pieces could not drown the snores of an Ohio hobo, escaping the howling gale outside and thus swelling the audience by one third. No time or energy for a visit to the Museum of Rock and Roll or to sample a swift half at the Grog Shop, Cleveland's premiere guitar venue. No sleep till Manhattan.

On Wednesday the sixteenth he drove a rented automatic Oldsmobile, expertly, from the heart of Boston through Frost and Dickinson country to Amherst where he was treated and toasted by the poet James Tate and his friends and accomplices. On Thursday the seventeenth he read to two hundred students at the University of Massachusetts, then floated back to the hotel five miles high, several sheets to the wind, and one suitcase lighter, courtesy of a determined sales pitch designed to relieve his aching back rather than fatten his wallet. At the Lord Jeffrey Inn he was brought back to earth with his twenty-seventh burst of static electricity of the tour, emanating this time from the handle of the toilet. He let out a cry of 'Fuck, Fuck' which must have startled the night-porter three floors below. By way of convalescence he took to his bed, only to be met by a further thwack of several thousand megawatts discharging from the bedside light and through his wedding ring, causing him to jump to his ailing feet and issue a string of similar oaths and obscenities.

On Friday the eighteenth, still buttoned to the bridge of his nose in an anorak sporting the slogan 'Expedition Antarctica' he touched down in sixty degrees of New York sunshine. The Mansfield Hotel on West 44th Street had kept its prices at rock bottom, he concluded, by cutting back on those optional extras one occasionally associates with hotel accommodation, such as vermin control and glass in the windows. At short notice he upgraded to a more splendid venue.

On Saturday the nineteenth and Sunday the twentieth he did everything that his postcards said he did, postcards that were penned in the White Horse Tavern each evening under a portrait of Dylan Thomas. Such circumstances and surroundings clearly led him to think a great deal of himself.

On Monday the twenty-first from the BBC studios above Rockefeller Plaza he delivered the poetry of various American poets into bedsits all over Britain via a telephone link-up with Radio One, broadcast from Manchester's Palace of Glittering Delights. Being tired, weary, and not a little homesick, he enquired as to the most recent performance of his luckless football team, and was grateful to a listener from Mirfield who called in to give a full and frank report of the latest match. That night, New York's small but thriving Huddersfield community were once again plunged into deep grief and uncontrollable frustration, and the streets were an angry place.

The business meetings of Tuesday the twenty-second passed off quietly but only with the help of two paracetamols on the hour every hour, and Wednesday the twenty-third was lost in a cloud of snow and a catalogue of cancelled flights.

On Thursday the twenty-fourth, following a false start reminiscent of the 1993 Grand National, and a stewards' enquiry at Heathrow Immigration Control, he finally glided into Manchester, shabby and unshaven like a travelling salesman but pleased to have demonstrated his samples and exported a selection of his goods. He exited the concourse with his head still in the clouds but his heart back in its rightful place, on the left, along with the traffic and a waiting car.

Brighton Festival of Literature & Debate   May 6-30   1994

Kindred Spirits explores the family: from biologial families, through tribes and nations, to artistic affinities.
New Generation Poets: **Simon Armitage, Lavinia Greenlaw & David Dabydeen** with **Melvyn Bragg** May 10
Smuggled Lines: **Grete Tartler & Fleur Adcock** May 13
Poems from the Pulpit: **Peter Porter** May 13 **& Jon Stallworthy** May 20
Life & Love in Luton: **John Hegley** May 20
Talking Bleeding Liberties: **Craig Raine** May 7
In and & Out of Danger: **James Fenton** May 21
Carol Ann Duffy at Charleston May 26
Europe in Ruins: **Hans Magnus Enzensberger** May 11
East & West: **Vikram Seth** May 19

For further details and free 20-page Literature Brochure, ring 0273 713875/6/7

KATHLEEN JAMIE
The Queen of Sheba

KATHLEEN JAMIE WAS BORN IN 1962 IN RENFREWSHIRE. SHE WON A GREGORY AWARD AT NINETEEN, publishing her first collection, *Black Spiders* (Salamander Press, 1982) a year later. In 1986 she co-wrote *A Flame in your Heart* (Bloodaxe) with Andrew Greig, and in 1987 published *The Way We Live* (Bloodaxe). She has travelled widely, publishing a prose book – *The Golden Peak* (Virago, 1992) – and *The Autonomous Region* (Bloodaxe, 1993), a collection of poems and photographs (by Sean Mayne Smith). *The Queen of Sheba* (Bloodaxe, 1994) is reviewed by Edwin Morgan on page 17.

Kathleen Jamie's verse is characterized by an exuberant independence of mind, formal fluency and an insatiable appetite for new experience. In the title poem of *The Way We Live* she celebrates 'endless gloaming in the North ... Asiatic swelter/... launderettes, anecdotes, passions and exhaustion,/Final Demands and dead men' – a short list of her typical concerns. Travel is a both an influence and subject of her work, and while her urge to journey may be romantic in impulse – 'Just sail. And keep sailing. Sail over the/edge if you must' – her descriptions of foreign lands are determinedly non-exotic. It is in the crowded context of real life that her revelations occur: 'the mind can ... chat blithely/about mountains, until/the last moment, that appalling rise that ends/in total unemotional blue'. Her love poems are strikingly unaffected, ranging from the fatalist sigh of 'Things that shall never be' to the strictly blissful: 'Canary that I am, caged and hung/from the eaves of the world/to trill your praise'. A crucial aspect of her poetry is the light which her travels shed on her country of origin. 'The Queen of Sheba' finds the eponymous heroine sashaying down Presbyterian aisles, brazen in the face of small-town Scotland's chary underachievement, while 'The Republic of Fife' and 'Dream of the Dalai Lama on Skye' shade in the local/global overlap with characteristic humour and humanity. Jamie is ambivalent about her own social history (eg. 'School Reunion'), but her uncertainty is poetically productive. There is an unusually strong sense of personal and artistic evolution in her work which inspires confidence for the future. **(KJ)**

Kathleen Jamie writes:
What can I say? I'm thirty-one, and have been writing for half of my life. Now I'm staring at this piece of paper trying to tell something about that writing and that life, without sounding portentous. For the ~~fifth~~ sixth time I tear it up and start again.

I got into university, with difficulty, and studied philosophy. Before that, there was my family, home and school – I remember kicking very hard against the small options which seemed to be our lot, as though I'd glimpsed a huge world but felt it was being withheld from me. Nowadays I feel part of it. Maybe my poems are the place where I make exchanges with the world. There are figures in much of my work; queens, princesses, wandering monks. I think

these are forms of energy; or aspects of the self, like the figures on tarot cards. I think my work is a means of exploration for me. Some explorations result in dead-ends.

I can't answer the question 'why do you write?' In bursts of enthusiasm I have tried to be a 'woman writer' and a 'Scottish writer' but grow irritated and feel confined. I have no motives, certainly no 'message', but I would like to write some very good poems.

(Reproduced, with permission, from *Dream State* (Polygon, 1994) – reviewed p. 22)

Three influential 20th C. books:
Rainer Maria Rilke, *Duino Elegies*; John Berryman, *The Dream Songs*; Elizabeth Bishop, *Collected Poems*.

THREE POEMS BY KATHLEEN JAMIE

Mr and Mrs Scotland are Dead

On the civic amenity landfill site,
the coup, the dump beyond the cemetry
and the 30-mile-an-hour sign, her stiff
old ladies' bags, open mouthed, spew
postcards sent from small Scottish towns
in 1960: Peebles, Largs, the rock-gardens
of Carnoustie, tinted like angelica in the dirt.
Mr and Mrs Scotland, here is the land you were dealt:
fair but cool, showery but nevertheless,
Jean asks kindly; the lovely scenery;
in careful school-room script –
The Beltane Queen was crowned today.
But Mr and Mrs Scotland are dead.

Couldn't he have burned them? Released
in a grey curl of smoke
this pattern for a cable knit? Or this:
tossed between a toppled fridge
and sweet-stinking anorak: *Dictionary for Mothers*
M:– Milk, *the woman who worries . . .;*
And here, Mr Scotland's John Bull Puncture Repair Kit;
those days when he knew intimately
the thin roads of his country, hedgerows
hanged with small black brambles' hearts;
and here, for God's sake, his last few joiners' tools,
SCOTLAND, SCOTLAND, stamped on their tired handles.

Do we take them? Before the bulldozer comes
to make more room, to shove aside
his shaving brush, her button tin.
Do we save this toolbox, these old-fashioned views
addressed, after all, to Mr and Mrs Scotland?
Should we reach and take them? And then?
Forget them, till that person enters
our silent house, begins to open
to the light our kitchen drawers,
and performs for us this perfunctory rite:
the sweeping, the turning out.

(This poem won Third Prize in the 1993 National Poetry Competition – see page 116)

One of Us

We are come in a stone boat,
a miracle ship that steers itself
round skerries where guillimots
and shags stand still as graves.
Our sealskin cloaks are clasped
by a fist-sized penanular brooch,
our slippers are feathery
guga's necks: so delicate
we carried them over the wracky shore,
past several rusted tractors. Truth:
this was a poor place, a
ragged land all worn to holes. No-one,
nothing, but a distant
Telecom van, a bungalow
tied with fishing floats
for want of flowers.

              That August night
the Perseid shower rained
on moor and lily-loch, on a frightened world
– on us, in a roofless sheiling
with all our tat: the
golden horn of righteousness,
the justice harp; what folks expect.
We took swans' shape
to cross the Minch, one last fling
with silly magic – at our first
mainland steps a dormobile
slewed into a passing place; cameras flashed.
So we stayed high, surprised
a forester making aolean flutes
from plastic tubes – ,
he shared his pay. 'Avoid the
A9. For God's sake,
get some proper clothes.' We ditched
the cloaks, bought yellow
Pringle sweaters in Spean Bridge,
and house by safe house
arrived in Edinburgh. So far so
tedious: We all hold
minor government jobs, lay plans, and bide our time.

Boy in a Blanket

Frost had crept to the river
like deer: cold vapour rose
as we crossed by a split log

to the burning-place:
bells and tiny cymbals
winked like planets in the ash. But, ah,

wasn't everything pristine –
hills, river, a crimson-breasted bullfinch
cupped in a stark tree,

and the inn-keeper's boy,
crazy as a staircase,
shouted his few words of our language

from the family's home-made
verandah, fruit trees
shrunk back to a stone.

So too the next valley;
a 'herd combing the long hair
of his goats

showed us a spring; rags
of clothing rotted on twigs.
Downstream: a rope bridge,

a creaking mill, the house on stilts
of menstruating women
heavy with vines:

and girls, pipes tucked
in their belts
watched as we climbed the inn's stairs,

To work fast, before winter –
before the barefoot boy
in a blanket who'd followed us

put them to fright, and the bells
combs, reed-pipes, harvest songs,
and bright dresses

were hid in blackened rafters
or buried like seeds,
dormant till they imagined we'd gone.

Long Live the Queen

Edwin Morgan admires the restless spirit of Kathleen Jamie

Kathleen Jamie,
The Queen of Sheba,
Bloodaxe, £6.95,
ISBN 1 85224 284 1

The compressed incisiveness of the poems in Kathleen Jamie's first book, *Black Spiders* (1982), made an immediate impact, and five years later the blurb of her collection *The Way We Live* referred to her enthusiastically but dangerously as 'the most outstanding young woman poet now writing in Britain'. She has enough individuality, pith and nous to keep such publisher's hype in her pocket and get on with the job of writing good poems as and when she can, both during and in the intervals of extensive travels in Pakistan and Tibet. The Scottish and the exotic meet in her work in a very productive way, and both are in evidence in her latest book.

The splendidly boisterous title-poem opens the collection and this Queen surely joins Carol Ann Duffy's Mrs Midas and Liz Lochhead's La Corbie as the most striking recent presentations of female characters by female poets. Conservative, suspicious, reductive Scotland has invoked her name ('Whae dis she think she is – the Queen o' Sheba?) too often, and now the real Queen has arrived, gorgeously sensual, trailing spices, showing her hairy legs, leading her swaying caravan of camels counter-clockwise round the kirkyaird, eating avocados with apostle spoons, ready with some warm hard questions for this cold northern promontory:

> she's shouting for our wisest
> man to test her mettle:

> Scour Scotland for a Solomon!

> Sure enough from the back of the crowd
> someone growls:
> *Whae do you think y'ur?*

> and a thousand laughing girls and she
> draw our hot breath
> and shout:

THE QUEEN OF SHEBA!

The engaging confidence of this put-down of dog-in-the-mangerism is a characteristic Jamie note, but it is not unaccompanied here by various sorts of restlessness and unease: a restlessness that either comes from or gives rise to her distant travels, an unease that seems to relate to the paradox we are so familiar with in 1990s Scotland – emphatic cultural presence coupled with total political impotence. In 'Den of the old men', she wonders if the pensioners clacking dominoes in their hut ought to build a raft 'and sail away, the lot of yez, / staring straight ahead / like captains'. And in 'The Republic of Fife', citizens in the past have dangled over a motorway to paint PAY NO POLL TAX on a flyover but are urged also to balance on a house-roof to get a (precarious) wider view:

> carefully stand and see
> clear to the far off mountains,
> cities, rigs and gardens

> Europe, Africa, the Forth and Tay bridges,
> even dare let go, lift our hands
> and wave to the waving citizens
> of all those other countries.

But Jamie is also a poet of the moment perceived, the incident noted, as some poems here show very finely, and at times enigmatically. In 'Fountain', she suddenly subverts criticism of the cheap glitzy artificiality of a shopping mall's coin-filled fountain by crying: 'Who says / we can't respond; don't still feel, / as it were, the dowser's twitch / up through the twin handles of the buggy'. There's another buggy in 'Child with pillar box and bin bags', where a young

mother photographs her baby on the dark side of a city street, we are not told why, while the sun shines on 'the other side of the street to that she'd chosen, / if she'd chosen or thought it possible to choose'. The intersection of the ordinary and the strange is beautifully dealt with in 'Sad bird': a solitary pigeon with drooping head is seen for two nights on a neighbouring roof, yellowed, in streetlight like an ornament, then gone; was it really sad, or sick, or resting in migrations, or were the human watchers projecting sadness onto it? – 'a small grief, precise / as a drug, measured and dropped / into the bird's plain thought'.

The fact that most of the fully achieved poems appear to be congregated in the first half of the book may leave a slight impression of letdown, as if the startling promise of the title-poem could not be sustained; but this would be unfair. The long five-page poem towards the end, 'School reunion', a departure into a more dislocated, cinematic style, may not be wholly convincing, but shows a mind eager to explore, and emitting many sparks on the way.

This collection, mostly in English, some of it in Scots, some in a mixture of the two, is a caravan of pleasures and insights and will be widely enjoyed.

DON PATERSON
Nil-Nil

DON PATERSON WAS BORN IN DUNDEE IN 1963. HE LEFT SCHOOL AT SIXTEEN AND HAS WORKED AS a professional jazz musician, living in London and Brighton. He came to the fore in *Poetry Review*'s 'New Poets 90' issue (Autumn, 1990), receiving a Gregory Award in the same year. His first collection, *Nil-Nil* (Faber) was published in 1993. He is currently Writer-in-Residence at Dundee University. His poem 'A Private Bottling' won first prize in the 1993 Arvon Poetry Competition.

The title poem of *Nil-Nil* expresses one of Paterson's recurrent themes – the irretrievability of things past. The poem is a jaundiced stroll through the hinterlands of memory in which the past is painted as a long scoreless draw; its blend of big ideas and football small-talk is characteristic of Paterson. The search for what-is-lost assumes grotesque proportions in his hysterico-comic epic, 'The Alexandrian Library' in which the poet rummages through a lifetime of marginalia, mental junk mail. Paterson's gift of wit is everywhere apparent. At times he expresses a kind of jaunty nihilism ('This is/Planck-Time/Absolute Zero/Albedo Fuck-All'), discharging Baudelairean bile, but he is just as likely to wind his way through labyrinthine narrative à la Borges or adopt an omniscient persona in order to meditate on *belle lettres* (see Aussemain's Pensées on p. 20). His work succeeds most emphatically when both strains are thoroughly mixed, as in 'The Ferryman's Arms': the poem is a grim thriller in which the poet 'takes himself on' at pool, emerging victorious and, simultaneously in the form of his doppelganger, vanquished.

Paterson is determinedly true to his Scottish working class background: while 'An Elliptical Stylus' is a clever piece of class polemic – quarrelling equally with snobs and liberals – he more frequently proves his case by presenting images of the everyday: eg, the sticky lino and zoo smell of Blind Annie Spall's flat in 'Amnesia' or the bodged withdrawal and subsequent fatherhood-by-default of 'Seed'. The sussed, terrace-wise quality of his language at first disguises the fact that Paterson has an unusually advanced sense of poetry as artifice. The tension in his work between matter-of-factness and sophisticated make-believe surfaces interestingly in his poems about love and sex: one moment he is imagining his perfect, geography-defying, train journey – the next he is unflinchingly recording the 'dry rut' of bad sex. There is a *driven* quality to Paterson's verse which sets him aside from more even-tempered practitioners of the craft, a passionate scepticism fuelling both his tomfoolery and his fits of philosophy; the sign of the 'real writer' is on him. **(KJ)**

Don Paterson writes:
Hi. My name's Don. I'm a Scorpio. I hate doing this. One day I'd like to be famous enough to just not do it, rather than spend 200 words telling you why I don't want to. The reason I don't want to talk about my poetry is because I don't consider my own remarks to be more relevant or interesting than anyone else's; this isn't so much humility as an abdication of responsibility, but a poem has to generate its own context and its own illumination. If it can't, then hell mend it, whether it's

your poem or my poem. As far as a credo goes: technical considerations aside, bad poems generally try to offer solutions, while good poems leave a little more fear, chaos, wonder or mystery in the world than there was before.

Three influential 20th C. books: Toss-up between Louis MacNeice's *Collected Poems*, Elizabeth Bishop's *Collected Poems*, Seamus Heaney's *Door into the Dark* and Paul Muldoon's *Why Brownlee Left*.

THREE POEMS BY DON PATERSON

Prologue

A poem is a little church, remember,
you, its congregation, I, its cantor;

so please, no flash, no necking in the pew,
or snorting just to let your neighbour know

you get the clever stuff, or eyeing the watch,
or rustling the wee poke of butterscotch

you'd brought to charm the sour edge off the sermon.
Be upstanding. Now: let us raise the fucking *tone*.

Today, from this holy place of heightened speech
we will join the berry-bus in its approach

to that sunless pit of rancour and alarm
where language finds its least prestigious form.

Fear not: this is spiritual transport,
albeit the less elevated sort;

though the coach will limp towards its final stage
beyond the snowy graveyard of the page,

no-one will leave the premises. In hell
the tingle-test is inapplicable,

though the sensitives among you may discern
the secondary symptoms: light sweats, heartburn,

that sad thrill in the soft part of the instep
as you crane your neck to weigh up the long drop.

In the meantime, we will pass round the Big Plate
and should it come back slightly underweight

you will learn the meaning of the Silent Collection,
for our roof leaks, and the organ lacks conviction.

My little church is neither high nor broad,
so get your heads down. Let us pray. Oh God

From *François Aussemain: Pensées*

One of the great advantages of a steadily deteriorating hand is that I frequently find myself mistaking one word for another; since only the rough contour of the word is preserved, it is invariably taken for one of its acoustic, rather than semantic, cognates. In the composition of verse, this small triumph of sound over meaning often results in a dramatic improvement of the text, if we remember that it is Euterpe and not Urania that we are, on these occasions, attempting to propitiate. The forces involved are easily identified: the invisible line along which I work exerts a gravitational pull on the written line that increases with the rapidity and freedom of its execution. The first line is, of course, Babel, the rushing river from which all tongues emerge, and to which all tongues will eventually return; the written line is a series of commonly agreed divagations from the fixed path, carefully exaggerated so as to make their shape unequivocal. When the latter expresses its nostalgia for the former, a mildly lunatic intrusion results. Uncontrolled, this would lead immediately to chaos, the interchangeability of all sounds; but if these interruptions could somehow be made selectively – that is to say, if we knew precisely when to let the pen speak, when the line – all the works of Dante and Ovid would be as vulgar jingles beside the very least of our own. This is plainly absurd, but there is, however, another solution, based on the following axiom: for an oracular utterance to have any practical application, its interpretation must be made within the context of the original enquiry. Given that the oracle is the pen, the context language, and the petitioner myself, I began to compose my poetry in the following fashion (I say *compose,* but in truth it soon became a purely hermeneutic activity): I would draw a line, with reasonable speed and as straight as I dared, from one side of the page to the other. From this, with a little practice, I could deduce my own secret intentions by choosing the words that imitated most closely the unconscious waverings of the hand, thus subjecting my spontaneous utterances to calculated mediation. (Attempts to render the same lines in both English and Latin proved astonishing – though many of the words were etymologically disparate, the broad sense, with very few exceptions, remained identical.) Soon, I found I could dispense with my own contribution altogether, and was able to discern the private monograms nascent in the line of a wave breaking on the shore, or in the rough serrature of a paper-tear. Predictably, they made for dull reading; only a fool, I thought, would claim to descry, in the grain of a lath of apple-wood, the little songs and griefs of the dead maelid. Then it struck me, that as a mere instrument of nature's will myself, I was helplessly attuned to the song of the pen, not that of the scribe. Mercifully I had only to make one change in the procedure to correct this: I reverted to the very oldest tongues, those that had not strayed too far from their mimetic origins: Old Lithuanian, Basque, and my childhood Brezonek, all transliterated to Roman script. I experienced something of the same joy one feels, when, viewing the moon through a telescope, the image is pulled sharply into focus, and the blurred disc resolves as a perfect sphere of pale seas and dark sierras. Now, from the tiny deviations in the hawk's flight and the hound's course, I have begun to uncover not only their own secret signatures, but the ancient and eternal fictions of which they are only the unwitting guardians, the vibrant quills that rest lightly in the hand of Nature herself. Given time, there will only one task left to us: to dream the high truths and monstrous profanities that are to be read in the invisible tracks we ourselves inscribe, century after century, in the inconstant elements.

11:00 Baldovan

Base Camp. Horizontal sleet. Two small boys
have raised the steel flag of the 20 terminus:

me and Ross Mudie are going up the Hilltown
for the first time ever on our own.

I'm weighing up my spending power, the shillings,
tanners, black pennies, florins with bald kings,

the cold blazonry of a half-crown, threepenny bits
like thick cogs, making them chank together in my pockets.

I plan to buy comics,
sweeties, and magic tricks.

However, I am obscurely worried, as usual,
over matters of procedure, the protocol of travel,

and keep asking Ross the same questions:
where we should sit, when to pull the bell, even

if we have enough money for the fare,
whispering, *Are ye sure? Are ye sure?*

I cannot know the little good it will do me;
the bus will let us down in another country

with the wrong streets and streets that suddenly forget
their names at crossroads or in building-sites

and no one will have heard of the sweets we asked for
and the man will shake the coins from our fist onto the counter

and call for his wife to come through, come through and see this
and if we ever make it home again, the bus

will draw into the charred wreck of itself
and we will enter the land at the point we left off

only our voices sound funny and all the houses are gone
and the rain tastes like kelly and black waves fold in

very slowly at the foot of Macalpine Road
and our sisters and mothers are fifty years dead.

Caledonia Dreaming

The Scottish poet W. N. Herbert has a poem, 'Mappamundi', which wittily suggests that Ireland has cornered the poetry market. He may have to rewrite it now, because Scottish poetry has triumphed in the New Generation. **Douglas Dunn** *celebrates:*

Seven Scots out of twenty poets chosen for the New Generation Poets publicity exercise is an agreeable score. It should feel good, too, for John Burnside, Robert Crawford, Carol Ann Duffy, W.N. Herbert, Mick Imlah, Kathleen Jamie and Don Paterson. It could even turn out to be significant for Scottish poetry as a whole. Although far from overbearing, its eminence has stemmed from the seniority of some its citizens. Norman MacCaig, Sorley Maclean, Edwin Morgan, George Mackay Brown, Derick Thomson and Iain Crichton-Smith don't behave like a gerontocracy, but when you add to the list major figures who died in the last fifteen years or so – MacDiarmid, Sydney Goodsir Smith, Robert Garioch and W.S. Graham, then something of the weight, as well as the intensities of Scottish Poetry in this century can be measured for the remarkable phenomena that they are. Acknowledgement of the fact outside Scotland is relatively rare,

Indigenously, there's been a lot to go on. There have been living monuments to accept or reject; the materials necessary to interior argument and creative self-definition have not been in short supply. Younger writers have been obliged to come up with clearer ideas of what they want, and if local examples don't provide it then the eclecticism of some of them indicate where answers might be found – America, Europe, Ireland, and England.

What Europeans call 'the middle generation' has played its part too. Kenneth White, Stewart Conn, Tom Leonard and Liz Lochhead, for example, show their own departures from the generation before them. From White's widely-travelled philosophical speculations, Conn's domestic lyricism, to the demotic and satirical poetry of Leonard and Lochhead, is to cover a lot of literary ground. A successful woman poet with a prominent public profile must have given heart to the younger women now writing and publishing.

Six of the Scots selected for the NGP promotion appear in Daniel O'Rourke's anthology *Dream State*. The exception is Mick Imlah whose 'Goldilocks' is at least as good as the best poems in the anthology. No doubt he'll survive an oversight that can barely have been calculated on the grounds of enfeebled nationality. A contrast of aboriginal 'working-class' and cultivated Scottishness is what 'Goldilocks' is about.

Dream State: *The New Scottish Poets* **Edited by Daniel O'Rourke,** **Polygon, £7.95** **ISBN 0 7486 6169 7**

Carol Ann Duffy and John Burnside both left Scotland as children, Moving from Glasgow to Stafford, Duffy remembers 'trying to change my accent to sound like the English kids'. John Burnside recollects 'being uprooted from my community, and from the dialect and local landscape of Fife'. In 'Originally', Duffy echoes a cry from childhood, *'I want our own country'*. In another poem she says, 'I am homesick, free, in love with the way my mother speaks'. These are more plangently straightforward disclosures than what arise from Burnside's questioning and thoughtful re-visits. 'But what we recognize is what we bring', he says in 'Out of Exile'. It could be a stricter use of experience. In its different way, though, it is the equal of Duffy's candour.

As the poet-critic of the group Robert Crawford has found his work described as 'academic'. Although the tag is blatant nonsense, his poetry depends on explicit cultural references within a self-aware framework of nationality. He tries to round up and recommend the constituent parts of an encyclopedic country. There can be a sense of inventory-making about it as well as a relish for detail. Neither tendency helps him achieve a recognizably lyrical mode, which probably interests him less than the positive excitement through which much of his writing is delivered: 'To be miniaturized is not small-minded./To love you needs more details than the/ Book of Kells/Your harbours, your photography, your/democratic intellect/Still boundless, chip of a nation'. Loud, clear, lively and hopeful, it is also impatient with regret, time-wasting, or what Auden called 'grate-gazing'.

Much the same could be said of W. N. Herbert's poetry in Scots. 'My writing wouldn't work until I reproduced the gull-like tones of my origins', he says. 'In Scots I pretend that my basic speech – Dundonian – hasn't been atrophied by cultural neglect, and still has access to the broad vocabulary of the Scots dictionary'. Note that 'pretend', though. Does it disable a poet's language when he or she has to 'pretend' that it actually exists? Probably not when what Herbert means by 'access' is proved by his poetry. He says that his enabling belief 'creates the language of a quasi-fictional country, one which offers a critique of the present status of "Scotland"'. A country which has to be named in inverted commas would seem to be in a bad way – under-defined, non-specific, dreamt, 'quasi-fictional', or in a bit of a state however you look at it. Perhaps the truth of the matter is that Scotland as reflected by its younger poets is not just diverse but perceived as hospitable to transformation. As old, rancid prejudices related to gender, sexuality, religion, colour, class and nationality shiver and wither, that transformational example in the aesthetic realm could become paradigmatic of Scottish poetry. On the other hand, it looks like trying to wave a magic wand.

Scots expressions appear in Kathleen Jamie's poems as more than touchstones of an accent but less than the 'pretend' language of a quasi-fictional country. Like Crawford and Herbert she can opt for a defiantly celebratory approach to her subjects, as in 'The Republic of Fife' or 'The Way We Live'. She can also be pithily inventive:

See thon raws o flint arraheids
in oor great museums o antiquities
awful grand in Embro –
Dae 'ye near'n daur wunner at wur histrie?
Weel then, Bewaur!
The museums of Scotland are wrang.
They urnae arraheids
but a show o grannies' tongues...

Two women in a list of seven Scottish poets might not look like a fair share of the roster but it is a marked improvement over the past. In *Dream State* (where there are nine women out of twenty-five contributors) Elizabeth Burns remarks on 'the question of an identity for women working in what has been the mainly male domain of Scottish poetry'. It's an active issue in Scottish writing. In criticism of recent fiction it's been suggested that 'Scottish writer' is a masculine category and that women writers must therefore identify themselves outside the convenient descriptions of nationality.

Reversals of previous gender-tactics are matched by a confidence that encourages a candid naming and use of everyday experience together with uninhibited class consciousness and a wide imaginative range. Underlying qualities like these are evident in Don Paterson's poetry – the naming in 'Nil Nil', for example, or the filial narrative of 'An Elliptical Stylus.'

Dream State underlines the impressive qualities

of the seven Scottish poets enlisted by NGP. Vitality, liveliness and mischief come naturally to most of these writers. But the anthology also reveals what could be a weakness – a lack of interest in artistry, 'Phoney dilemmas every one', O'Rourke says in his introduction of some standard Scottish poetic dilemmas – one of them is 'free verse as opposed to rhyme'. It can be 'phoney' only if you make it that. Similarly, actual politics appear to be seen by most of the poets in *Dream State* as an avoidable chunk of frustration. Popular culture seems as potent a resource as political energy, although the two could be affiliated in a country where jazz, rock, the movies and 'style' have always been big. The-poet-as-performer might already have earned a place in popular culture, whether it's the only place for a poet to be is another question. Some of the best poems in the book (Raymond Friel's 'Schooldays', David Kinloch's 'Envoi: Warmer Bruder', Angela McSeveney's 'Night Shift', Iain Bamforth's 'Calvinist Geography') are remote from any expectations of performance and the audience-nudging that can go with it.

What these poets represent is a large change in Scottish poetry; but the breakthrough is mainly at the level of disclosure and personality. While these are part of what is usually meant by 'voice' (see, especially Jackie Kay's poems, or Graham Fulton's) their accomplishment seems diminished without the craft and artistry for which the raw interest of what is said is an incomplete compensation. But given the social obstacles in the way of occupying your own vocal space – issues such as gender, sexuality, skin colour, religion, class, language and accent – perhaps the real achievement of *Dream State* is that it should exist at all. Fulton's high-spirited but depressing 'Cream of Scottish Youth' rings all too true.

Tumbled

yelling, from dizzy swish roundabouts,
pelted the swans in the dam with cans,
tore the pages from the brainyboy's books
then tipped his schoolbag upside down,
lit fires just for the hell of it, splashed
scruffy steam gold against the oaks

that had seen it all before.

It's as true as Meg Bateman's love poems, or the gobstopping *schadenfreude* of Roddy Lumsden's 'The Misanthrope's Afternoon Walk', or the alleged boundlessness of the more positive Scottish qualities observed by Robert Crawford, William Hershaw's class and linguistic loyalties, or Anne C. Frater's Gaelic political jabs. But it wasn't always represented in poetry before now, even if fiction has been more conscientious in its struggles with social realities,

Does it all betoken a 'renaissance'? Not really. Promotions of the NGP kind, and anthologies of younger poets, can leave the picture looking incomplete. The accusation is not that such enterprises are ageist but that a temporary emphasis on just part of a country's literature can leave it appearing to suffer from deficiencies where these might not be the case. Those (happily) long-lived and productive older generations signify the real renaissance of Scottish poetry. *Dream State* shows a heartening continuation of inventiveness and expressive courage. What's missing, though – and I regret this – is an aesthetic dedication comparable to MacCaig's, Brown's, Smith's, Morgan's, or Maclean's. There is also an aftertaste of a generation only slightly older being hard done by, poets like Andrew Greig, Tom Pow, Angus Martin, Frank Kuppner and John Glenday. There's solid talent there, too.

Two or three poets absent from *Dream State* might have felt that they'd a reasonable claim to be included – Hugh McMillan, for example, or Margaret

Fulton Cook. But in terms of numbers alone the upsurge of younger talent in Scottish poetry is remarkable. When you look back to what poetry was like in Scotland in the early 1960s the contrast is so stark that it is difficult even to make it. A lot has changed, for the better. It might even be worth mentioning that at least some of the credit falls to the Scottish Arts Council's Literature Department, which has never had to suffer damaging policies imposed from above. Over a sustained period it has been able to support writers with Fellowships, bursaries, and subsidies to publishers and editors as well as its Writers in Schools and Writers in Public programmes. These activities form an indispensable plank of the Scottish literary economy,

The real renaissance in Scotland has to be seen in broader terms. It includes fiction, drama and criticism as well as poetry. Indeed, it includes all the arts. Poetry and other kinds of writing have been reacting to, feeding from, nurturing and being nourished by animated cultural and political scenes. All we need now is a football team.

RON BLUFF WRITES:

FARQUHARSON CAIRNS is one of the 'Lab Boys', a group of US-influenced Scottish experimental poets associated with the magazine *K=I=R=K=C=A=L=D=Y*. 'Barc Ode' from Cairns's third collection *Li Po Oildrums* (Bloab, 1990) is something of a manifesto piece. Interviewed in *National Spindle* (May 1992) Cairns explained: 'I wanted a work that was fully machine-readable, yet also a homage to Hugh MacDiarmid. Where MacDiarmid rifled dictionaries, I plunder the shelves of Tesco and Safeway'. Born, Cairns began his career as a site-specific sculptor on Tiree, but most of his works were destroyed in the 1980s to make way for passing places on the island's road. He came to prominence in *Poetry Review*'s 'New Tiree Poets' issue (Vol 62 No 3 – copies still available) and was immediately the subject of exams at UCLA and the Sorbonne. He has since been writer-in-residence at the Leith Pizza Hut and has served a short sentence for spitting on Radio 4's *Kaleidoscope*. In *Le Supermarché du Texte* Jacques

Barc Ode

Baugraullad has written of 'Barc Ode': 'Farquharson Cairns est un poète très ovidien; son oeuvre est metamorphique, en veilleuse entre le monde organique et le checkout fnac'. Professor Louise Stargazer, author of *Farquharson Cairns: A Deconstructive Critique*, sees 'Barc Ode' as a 'liminal work, mediating between late-20th-century multi-national capital and primitive totemism; fusing the texture of tree bark with the flutings of the doric column, merchandizing with arboriculture, it exposes contradictions at the foundations of our western metaphysic'. At the same time, the poem can be seen as an ironic commentary on the 'Language' anthology, *In the American Tree*. Cairns has pronounced himself delighted with his inclusion in the NEW GENERATION POETS promotion: 'I think it is highly significant that of the twenty poets selected, twenty-one are Scottish'.

DAVID DABYDEEN
Turner

DAVID DABYDEEN WAS BORN IN 1955 IN GUYANA AND RAISED ON A SUGAR PLANTATION (THE majority of Guyanese work on sugar estates owned until recently by the British company Booker, of literary prize fame). He read English at Cambridge and London Universities, completing his doctorate in 1982. He is now Director of the Centre for Research into Asian Migrations at the University of Warwick, and Guyana's Ambassador-at-large. His first book, *Slave Song* (Dangaroo, 1984) won the Commonwealth Poetry Prize. *Coolie Odyssey* followed from Dangaroo in 1988. He has also written two novels, *The Intended,* and *Disappearance*, both from Secker & Warburg in 1991, and several critical books. *Turner* (Cape) is reviewed by Margaret Busby on page 30.

David Dabydeen's first book was written entirely in Creole and he has been a powerful advocate of the oral culture of the West Indies (see 'Dreadtalk', *Poetry Review*, Winter 1990-91). The poems in *Slave Song* are all concerned with the harsh life of the canecutters, its deprivations and abuses. *Coolie Odyssey* uses mostly standard English and in the title poem explicitly takes on Heaney and Harrison: 'Now that the peasantry is in vogue,/Poetry bubbles from peat bogs, People strain for the old folks fatal gobs/Coughed up in grates North or North east'. In 'Turner' the language vies with the bravura technique of Turner's painting. It is a poem raised from a howling gap: the severance of life in Africa, the easy severance of lives flung into the sea, the gap between salon appreciation of Turner's pigments and the drowned African in the picture's foreground. Towards the end he invokes Eliot: '... time future was neither time past/Nor time present, but a rupture so complete/That pain and happiness will become one ...'

David Dabydeen writes:

I grew up in the Caribbean on English words but no corresponding English images apart from a 'Bless This House' print of Jesus pinned over our bed which I would stare at for hours in periods of illness. If in later life I dabbled in art history it must have originated in those moments when a feverish child, between one asprin and another, fastened on to the only picture on the wall. Jesus looked like Superman (Guyana was coming under American influence and we were being exposed to American literature). Both were white, though English Jesus had long hair and a kindlier face. Both had emblematic hearts inscribed on their chests. I knew I'd meet both one day, as boys do.

In the 1960s the Americans invaded our country with money and guns, and we fled Superman and arrived in England. Instead of Jesus I met Hogarth, and it was England that was sick this time. All that homelessness, unemployment, rioting and recession! All those whores and syphilitic children being abused by the Whig and Tory rich! I then met Turner who had turned a blind eye to such messiness and faced the sea instead but who still couldn't get away from the reality of blood and catastrophe. Hence all those shipwrecks, Belgranos and incarnadine waves. Hogarth and Turner: the only two great artists that England produced. With the Gawain poet, Hardy, Conrad and Lawrence they've taken up most of my studious time in England. Whenever England appears Larkinesque and dull of motion, flaunting its own cruelty and darkness, it is the fierce transfigurative energy of these artists I wish to celebrate.

DAVID DABYDEEN

Extract from: *Turner*

XII

The sea has brought me tribute from many lands,
Chests of silver, barrels of tobacco, sugar-loaves,
Swords with gleaming handles, crucifixes set in pearls
Which, marvelled at, but with the years grown rusty
And mouldy, abandoned – cheap and counterfeit
    goods:
The sea has mocked and beggared me for centuries,
Except for scrolls in different letterings
Which, before they dissolve, I decipher
As best I can. These, and the babbling
Of dying sailors, are my means to languages
And the wisdom of other tribes. Now the sea
Has delivered a child sought from the moon in years
Of courtship, when only the light from that silent
Full eye saw me whilst many ships passed by
Indifferently. She hides behind a veil
Like the brides of our village but watches me
In loneliness and grief for that vast space
That still carries my whisper to her ears,
Vaster than the circumference of the sea
That so swiftly drowned my early cries
In its unending roar. There is no land
In sight, no voice carries from that land,
My mother does not answer, I cannot hear her
Calling, as she did when I dragged myself
To the bank of the pond, my head a pool
And fountain of blood, and she runs to me
Screaming, plucks me up with huge hands,
Lays me down on land, as the sea promised
In early days, clasped and pitched me sideways
In the direction of our village, my dazed mind
Thought, across a distance big beyond even
Turner's grasp (he sketches endless numbers
In his book, face wrinkled in concentration
Like an old seal's mouth brooding in crevices
Of ice for fish; like my father
Counting beads at the end of each day,
Reckoning which calf was left abandoned
In the savannah, lost from the herd, eaten
By wild beasts. He checks that we are parcelled

In equal lots, men divided from women,
Chained in fours and children subtracted
From mothers. When all things tally
He snaps the book shut, his creased mouth
Unfolding in a smile, as when, entering
His cabin, mind heavy with care, breeding
And multiplying percentages, he beholds
A boy dishevelled on his bed). For months
It seemed to speed me to a spot where my mother
Waited, wringing her hands, until I woke to find
Only sea. Months became years and I forgot
The face of my mother, the plaid cloth
Tied around her neck, the scars on her forehead,
The silver nose-ring which I tugged, made her start,
Nearly rolling me from her lap but catching me
In time, and when I cried out in panic
Of falling, pinned me tightly, always,
To her bosom. Now I am loosed
Into the sea, I no longer call,
I have even forgotten the words.
Only the moon remains, watchful and loving
Across a vast space.

XIII

Sometimes half her face grows dark, she sulks
Impatient of my arms, all my entreaties
Grappled in a storm of rain; nothing will soothe her
Then, she cries herself to sleep or curves
Like a sickle that will wake the sky's throat,
Or curls her lip in scorn of me, a mere unborn
With insufficient cowrie shells, when others,
Men, substantial, beseech her favours
With necklaces of coloured glass to loop
Around her breasts, men of presence, neither ghost
Nor portent of a past or future life
Such as I am, now. Sometimes her cheeks are puffed,
Her face lopsided, and I think I must have
Blasted her in some lover's rage; my hand,
Two centuries and more lifeless, clenched in quick
Hate, reached endlessly to bruise her face.
She disappears behind clouds for many nights.
A sudden thought writhes: she might be dead,
I might never subject her again.

XIV

It was not her going but the manner of it,
Like Turner's hand gripping my neck,
Pushing me towards the edge, that no noise
Comes from my mouth, no lamentation
As I fall towards the sea, my breath held
In shock until the waters quell me.
Struggle came only after depth, the flush
Of betrayal, and hate hardening my body
Like cork, buoying me when I should have sunk
And come to rest on the sea's bed among
The dregs of creatures without names
Which roamed these waters before human birth:
Jaws that gulped in shoals, demons of the universe
Now grin like clowns, tiny fish dart
Between the canyons of their teeth. I should have sunk
To these depths, where terror is transformed into
Comedy, where the sea, with an undertaker's
Touch, soothes and erases pain from the faces
Of drowned sailors, unpastes flesh from bone
With all its scars, boils, stubble, marks
Of debauchery.

XV

I gather it in with dead arms, like harvest-time
We trooped into the fields at first light,
The lame, the hungry and frail, young men
Snorting like oxen, women trailing stiff
Cold children through mist that seeps from strange
Wounds in the land. We float like ghosts to fields
Of corn. All day I am a small boy
Nibbling at whatever grain falls from
My mother's breast as she bends and weaves
Before the crop, hugging a huge bundle
Of cobs to her body, which flames
In the sun, which blinds me as I look up
From her skirt, which makes me reach like a drowning
Man gropes at the white crest of waves, thinking it
Rope. I can no longer see her face
In the blackness. The sun has reaped my eyes.
I struggle to find her in the blackness
At the bottom of the sea where the brightest
Sunken treasure barely keeps its glow.

Old English Creole

David Dabydeen, in an edited version of his recent Poets on Poets talk, on the anonymous fourteenth-century author of Sir Gawain and the Green Knight

The medieval age was the age of innocence. A peculiar description, considering the wars that raged, the system of serfdom, the diseases, the tyranny of the rich, the tyranny of men, the process of theft ('English history is a history of theft', Raymond Williams wrote, referring to the baronial squabble for lands). Still, for me, it was the age of innocence in that it was precolonial: they had nothing to do with me and I had nothing to do with them. I can read the literature of the period without engaging with ethnic or colonial issues. The sensation is one of an exhilarating freedom from the white man's burden.

Yet English medieval literature has intriguing connections with twentieth century Caribbean writing. Take the language of *Sir Gawain* – the muscular, lyrical, almost barbarous language of the north of England:

> Sithen the sege and th' assaut watz sesed at Troye
> The borgh that brittened and brent to brondes and askes

The *physical* process of destruction and catastrophe are enacted in the language. When I first read *Sir Gawain* I was instantly drawn back to the creolized English of my childhood, its brokenness, its harsh lyricism, its demotic energy, its revelling in alliterative sounds. Chaucer, a southerner and a courtier, poked fun at the 'rustic' language of *Sir Gawain*. Chaucer's iambic pentameter won the day, becoming the standard line in English poetry. Dryden and Matthew Arnold called Chaucer the Father of English Poetry, not the Gawain poet.

The tension between the English north and the English south has echoes of the tension between the Caribbean colonies and the imperial Mother Country. The challenge to Caribbean poets was how to shatter the frame of the iambic pentameter imposed upon us by the metropolis; how to write with a rhythm that approximated to the forces of *our* landscape. 'The hurricane does not roar in pentameters', as the Barbadian poet Edward Brathwaite put it. 'My feet is my only carriage', Bob Marley sang, and we have had to find our own poetic feet to carry us forward to a genuine independence.

It was the landscape of *Sir Gawain* which also impacted on my sense of Guyanese-ness. Outside the warmth, brightness and security of the medieval Court are the penumbral regions – hostile forests, and hostile animals – which Sir Gawain has to encounter and traverse. It is a primitive or original landscape. Present-day Guyana possesses the same feel of magic and originality. We live on a thin strip of coastland, wedged between the roaring Atlantic and the Amazonian jungle. The coastal strip is our island and oasis, our version of the protective Court. The landscape of natural disorder provokes awe but also an overwhelming feeling of peril. Rivers glide along for miles, then without announcement, drop several hundred feet in stupendous waterfalls, before continuing their passage at a different plane. There are plateaux – mountains without heads. Where did the heads go? There are stretches of pure white sand, complete with shells and other traces of ancient marine life, in the middle of the jungle, but no sea; the sea had washed in millions of years ago, then retreated, leaving beaches. The mysterious, threatening nature of the Guyanese landscape has been the ideal setting for the fictions of Conan Doyle, W.H. Hudson, Wilson Harris and others.

These days, with England reduced to a patchwork of fields and pin-stripe lawns, it's difficult to imagine the sheer physical threat posed by the Medieval landscape. The only wild life left in England are those creatures to be seen, in every street, at closing time. And, of course, the fox. Poor fox, hunted down relentlessly by English writers in pursuit of a primitive metaphor!

Which brings us to the Green Man. The Gawain Poet, influenced by Christianity, has tamed him somewhat. Elsewhere in Medieval writing however, the Green Man is monstrous and misbegotten, a symbol of our latent capacities for sexual mayhem ... the 'id', in Freudian terms. Over 600 years later, Conrad published a 'version' of the Gawain story, *Heart of Darkness*, in which it is the Black Man who satisfies the English need for a demonic other. The Green Man has become the Black Man in English demonology, the man who stands outside the pale of civilization and issues sexual and linguistic threats against that civilization.

What happened between the Medieval and the Modern period to effect such a change? The Empire.

The Slave Ship (detail)

Margaret Busby on *David Dabydeen*'s *poetic study of Art, Empire and Emancipation*

David Dabydeen,
Turner: New & Selected Poems,
Cape, £7.00,
ISBN 0 224 03895 8

At the New Generation Poets launch, David Dabydeen lamented the fact that there were not more of 'us' sharing the opportunity. He referred to poets such as Jackie Kay and Fred D'Aguiar, and I too feel disappointment that the strictures of competition processes worked against them this time. Dabydeen's concern is in line with the recurrent themes of his work, which deals unflinchingly with Black history as it affects the legatees of Empire both in the Caribbean and Britain.

The raw Creole cadences of the people of the canefields, the descendants of indentured East Indians and enslaved Africans, imbue his first two poetry collections: *Slave Song* (1984), and *Coolie Odyssey* (1988). This new collection, *Turner*, includes 20 poems from his previous collections (eight that use local patois have facing-page standard English 'translations'), but the impressive long title poem is by far his most ambitious yet. In a Preface, Dabydeen explains that it was inspired by a Turner painting exhibited at the Royal Academy in 1840, 'Slavers throwing overboard the dead and dying' (or 'The Slave Ship'): 'It was not unusual for ship captains to order the drowning of sick slaves (who would fetch a low price on landing in the Caribbean), and to claim their insurance values on the basis of goods lost at sea'.

Dabydeen's aim is to show the artist in a new light: 'The intensity of Turner's painting,' says Dabydeen, 'is such that I believe the artist in private must have savoured the sadism he publicly denounced'. The poem focuses on the submerged head of the African in the foreground of Turner's painting, which has been drowned in Turner's (and other artists') sea for centuries. When it awakens it can only partially recall the sources of its life, so it invents a body, a biography, and peoples an imag-ined landscape. Ultimately, however, the African rejects the fabrication of an idyllic past, but he is too trapped by memory to escape history. Although the sea has transformed him – bleached him of colour and complicated his sense of gender – his desire for transfiguration or newness or creative amnesia is frustrated. The agent of self-recognition is a stillborn child (named Turner, like the captain of the slaveship) tossed overboard from a future ship. The child floats towards him. He wants to give it life, to mother it, but the child – his unconscious and his origin is steeped in memory of ancient cruelty.

> 'Nigger' it cries, loosening from the hook
> Of my desire, drifting away from
> My body of lies. I wanted to teach it
> A redemptive song, fashion new descriptions
> Of things, new colours fountaining out of
> form,
> I wanted to begin anew in the sea
> But the child would not bear the future
> Nor its inventions, and my face was rooted
> In the ground of memory, a ground
> stampeded
> By herds of foreign men who swallow all its
> fruit
> And leave a trail of dung for flies
> To colonize; a tongueless earth, bereft
> Of song except to the idiot witter
> Of wind through a dead wood.

Stained indelibly by Turner's language and imagery, neither can escape Turner's representation of them as exotic and sublime victims.

There can be no happy ending to this tale of the Middle Passage, but a message for the scattered tribe chimes with Dabydeen's aims: that, stripped of adornment,

> each must learn to live
> Beadless in a foreign land; or perish ... Each
> Will be barren of ancestral memory
> But each endowed richly with such emptiness
> From which to dream, surmise, invent,
> immortalize.
> Though each will wear different coloured
> beads
> Each will he Manu, the source and future
> Chronicles of our tribe.

SUSAN WICKS
Open Diagnosis

SUSAN WICKS GREW UP IN KENT AND STUDIED FRENCH AT THE UNIVERSITIES OF HULL AND SUSSEX, where she wrote a D. Phil. thesis on the fiction of Andre Gide. She has taught in France, America and Ireland. She lives in Tunbridge Wells with her husband and two daughters, and works as a part-time tutor for the University of Kent. She was one of the featured poets in *Poetry Review*'s new poets issue, 'Jostling at the Sacred Gate', Autumn 1992. Her first collection, *Singing Underwater*, was published by Faber in 1992 and was shortlisted for the Eliot Prize. *Open Diagnosis,* was published by Faber in April this year and is reviewed by Ian McMillan on page 33.

In her two books, Susan Wicks has established a wholly distinctive voice. She shows an unusual empathy with creatures and has a curious, prophetic attitude to the people in her poems. The longest section of *Open Diagnosis* is a remarkable series of poems on multiple sclerosis. Like Sharon Olds, whom she admires, Susan Wicks is fully alert to the sad dance of matter, both radiant and diseased, as it passes through its transformations in people and outside them.

Her poems usually proceed in a measured way, accumulating their images carefully – 'Today the world is white and set'; 'It is about a girl standing on a staircase') – but occasionally she trips into plangent song and refrain: 'Child and willow, child and willow,/break me loose from the leaning trunk ...' Rhyme is used very rarely, but to great effect in 'Forgetting Hallsands' in *Singing Underwater*, a narrative about the loss to the sea of the village of Hallsands: Often she pursues a suggestion through fictional realms till it returns to illuminate the everyday: 'On an Error in Your Passport' has a baby born one year too early ('Four months later the sickness began'). In one of the key poems in *Open Diagnosis* the sickness is judged to have begun at birth: 'I have always/had an invisible limp,/ a peripheral numbness ...' – a moment of terrible revelation, both imprisoning and liberating. **(PF)**

Susan Wicks writes:
I think irony is still our best friend and worst enemy. I think we still want the luxury of being able to say, 'I am writing a poem', with an ironic twinkle in our eye. For me there is a kind of intellectual cowardice in that. If we aren't prepared to take emotional and aesthetic risks, not prepared to lay ourselves open to the dangers of sentimentality or melodrama, how can we expect our readers to be fully human and vulnerable as they read us?

I know that in some ways I've been more influenced by novelists than I have by poets. I often find myself more interested in criteria of tone, distance and reliability than I am in language for its own sake. I hope that in my best poems the 'language' almost

disappears. What I would like to achieve is a language that could make the reader read more slowly and attentively almost without his or her knowledge, and allow the connections in a poem to surface gradually.

To me the connections are all-important. In the end even the subjects don't matter very much. I care about them – *of course* – but what the poem cares about is something less personal.

Three influential 20th century books:

Apollinaire, *Alcools* (in the original French);
Sharon Olds, *The Dead and the Living;*
Gerald Stern, *The Red Coal.*

THREE POEMS BY SUSAN WICKS
Burgh Island, 1st September

I could stand here all night watching
the tide come in, where unknown children
squeal as the sea wraps them
in cold, and the next wave crawls towards us,
wriggles into footprints. I could
begin to admire God,
His repeats and ritual hesitations,
the lace of brown scum His slow fingers
have ravelled, His sliced shells and pebbles
in subtle calibrations as the sea stirs them
and leaves them, a whole castle
levelled to a streak. All night I could stand holding
the straps of my flapping sandals
till the land was a cold stroke in darkness
and the strait opened to my bare feet
in running furrows, the one causeway
narrowed to a spine of ripples
and the Island, its hotel, its sharp grasses,
cut off – till the sea tractor
lumbered out again to its harvest of water.

Landing

We meet on landings; outside the night
is furred with frost. You are warm,
sleepy as fruit, your peach satin
pyjamas rumpled, scented with breath.

Below us an old house
hums. Through windows the dark
is a net of trees, trapped stars.
Darling, in the cold airways

a woman flares like a phoenix, a child's hand
strikes blood from brick. Bodies
such as yours lie blackened, buckled
on hard shoulders. Sleepless,

I meet you, we cling to each other,
our hearts beat back gravity, feathered
in red juice like a split stone.

Your Baby

We were the ones who stole her,
took her from her pram unwitnessed,
peeled the damp clothes from her body.

We stroked her cheek raw with love,
combed out her rasp of tangles
to red silk, kept her nails in a casket.

We washed her soft creases, lulled her
with the pressure of fingers, wrapped her
in leaves. We knelt to feed her

to the dark. Now in this sunlit corridor
your thin breasts sag as you still cradle
an old doll. The synthetic features

worry your flesh, the tufted
hair stands out with longing. *Have you seen
my baby?* And we must answer

for this hard grey skin, these nails
perfect as shells, these limbs, this plastic slit
mouth that is beyond telling.

Measuring the Unfamiliar

by Ian McMillan

Susan Wicks,
Open Diagnosis,
Faber, £5.99, ISBN 0 571 17139 7

I bet you ten quid Susan Wicks could write great film scripts. Look at these descriptions, and imagine directors drooling over them: 'This/ is what dark is. Starlight/ turns my hair white as I crouch, pans gold in my small puddle' ('Bear Country'). Listen to these character notes: 'Dress carefully. Choose/ the faded childhood anorak,/ the torn skirt with the fringes./ Take a container for pennies, something to drape over you' ('How to Become Invisible'). How about this depiction of action: 'She might have been sleeping on a flat roof/ or making bread, or pounding the wet linen,/ her back turned to Him in an arched doorway,/ or singing as she walked home carrying water' ('First Coming'). These would have to be very special films, though: sunsurround, scratch 'n sniff, scratch 'n bleed: 'Tides of saliva sucked/ and fell, glinted at the edges/ of his laborious words./ When we were all finished, he still had a plateful/ to guide upwards with his good hand' ('Communion').

Much of the work here seems to want to leap from the page in a grown-up version of the pop-up book; at times it's as though Wicks is writing in a special three-dimensional ink the rest of us are denied access to, creating a yet-to-be-invented virtual reality interactive slim volume that lets you inhabit the poems like you inhabit certain kinds of sculpture. Read this and tell me I'm lying: 'At eight I already dreamed/ of breasts, full warm moons/ in eclipse like my mother's,/ her valley of skin, the unthinkable/ red blisters of sun-spots/ at each nipple, the buried blue rivers/ streaking the pale surfaces' ('Breast Envy').

Of course you could say that some of the things Susan Wicks writes about would be impossible to write about in a dull way, as in 'Seeing with Hands', about a child pretending to be blind –

She plays at Helen Keller,
measuring the unfamiliar
rooms, eyes shut, touching
their dark furniture.

She walks stumbling on treasure –
a stamp, a coin, a needle –
crouches with spread fingers,
breathing the floor's honey

– but I know that any poetry magazine editor will tell you from bitter experience that wonderful subjects are all too easily written about in a crushingly dull way. Wicks can use the tools of the trade well; she's absorbed, it seems to me, not only the classic poetic tradition (defined however you like) but also the lessons of the poets of the 'sixties, 'seventies and 'eighties so that like many of the NG poets, she's a real voice of the 'nineties.

She's very good on the dislocations of travel, an area that the prose writers with their big advances seem sometimes to have stolen from the poets – 'I catch myself on corners/ trying to look both ways: on a stranger's bicycle/ I circle endlessly/ before I can be sure of leaving/ in the appropriate direction'. She also excels at the illuminating anecdote, a method often attempted but not often pulled off – 'One day a man came to us/ with a small jar, asking permission/ to scatter his mother's ashes/ in the light that lay like dust/ between the rows of Red Gauntlet' ('Strawberry-picking') – and the telling visual detail: 'my father would bend to kiss me/ goodnight, the answer of his pale body/ swinging in the dark between us/ like a fish on a hook' ('Hangman'). Perhaps unfairly though, this book will be remembered for its vivid and moving poems about illness, a subject that's another trap for the unwary, but which Wicks tackles with unearthly skill: 'In the blue pool, her body/ was like anyone's, flattened as ours were/ by refraction, fish-pale, only the water/ making it monstrous. She swam/ almost as we swam, one leg trailing/ imperceptibly' ('Message From Galena'). The suffering becomes real poetry, in an almost impossibly moving way: 'I have always been/ this. I have always/ had an invisible limp,/ a peripheral numbness, always/ seen men tower over me, as if from a wheelchair' ('Coming Out'). If this book was a hand, it would be a beautiful, trembling one.

IAN DUHIG
The Bradford Count

IAN DUHIG WAS BORN IN LONDON IN 1954. IN 1987 HE WON FIRST PRIZE IN THE NATIONAL POETRY Competition with 'Nineteen Hundred and Nineteen' and has published widely in the UK and Ireland. His first book, *The Bradford Count*, was published by Bloodaxe in 1991 and reviewed by Ian McMillan in *Poetry Review*, Spring 1992; his second, *The Mersey Goldfish*, is due in 1995.

Although he was born in England, Duhig's parents were Irish Catholics and this ancestry informs his work. His blend of weird scholarship and boggy physicality is peculiar and quite unique. Ken Smith has described his work as 'gnarled, knuckled and – thank god – most unBritish'; this is true of the present day but singularly ignores the progenitor of 'modern' English poetry, Chaucer – with whom Duhig has an odd affinity. The Middle Ages is Duhig's favourite time-zone in *The Bradford Count*, a work in which vulgarity wrestles with muddy etymology and geo-political analysis. The result is often baffling – on a good page Duhig is obliquely illuminating and spectacularly entertaining; at worst he is merely spectacularly oblique. The award-winning 'Nineteen Hundred and Nineteen' stars Michael Robartes (of Yeatsian renown), with walk-on parts from Freud, Lenin, and 'a drunken madwoman in red skirts' – this against a backdrop of myth-laden Mexico. Such generation of multiple story lines and the ideological disinclination to knot them marks Duhig's poetry, as does his conspicuous sense of humour. The absurdly positioned missionary in 'Fundamentals' invites a belly-laugh – 'In many respects our God is not like your God./His name, for example, is not also our name for "rain"./Neither does it have for us the connotation "sexual intercourse"', yet the jaded aesthete of 'The Lady who Loved Insects' articulates a subtler amusement: 'He bored me with pillow books, gossamer diaries'. In the course of *The Bradford Count* Duhig hops from arcane folk lore to Welsh in-laws, skips from 12th century Ireland to 20th century Mexico and finally jumps into the lake with his copy of 'The Grey Psalter of Antrim' – 'Text completely illegible from this point/because of lake water and otter dung'. **(KJ)**

Ian Duhig writes:

When I was a teenager, O nearly a year ago now, one major ambition was to achieve the full fathom of manly stature. My eyes failed me. At my most erect they were still too close to the ground. If the tv was poor my parents would mock my atheism – the only man exactly six feet tall was Jesus Christ. At school they taught the Lateran Relics demonstrated He was five foot four. Clearly Our Saviour was unusually telescopic, even by the standard of His male image. In fact, I met nobody who knew this strange, Platonic folk-story of my parents and loved it for that. We shared a credibility gap, were but mortally telescopic. Recently, the Rathcoole Women's Litera-

ture Group through W.E.A. Northern Ireland invited me to read and discuss my poetry with them (they're hard these Protestants). It was great, a geg until one of them confirmed my parents' story. It swelled to six foot on the spot. Dead on. Now it fits my clothes better, is preferred by my wife to me and gives my son a closer run for his money on the megadrive. It is the real thing. Jesus Christ only ever had fat hair.

Three influential 20th C. books:

Derek Walcott, *In a Green Light; Poets from the North of Ireland*, (ed. Frank Ormsby); Adrian Rice *Muck Island*.

Do you feel a special poetic affinity with any of your

THREE POEMS BY IAN DUHIG
Estuary English

During the hundredth birthday of James Joyce
while on the tiles of a W.C.
I mused upon Irish economy;
the language has sacked its K, Q and X
yet the meaning of *whiskey*'s Kafkaesque;
in the cold bog of that Galway hotel
where all the world's newspapers are displayed
under glass like great ugly butterflies
I looked into my heart and my entrails
before the page of the *Wall Street Journal*
recording the poet Qin Guan's death
by drink – who forefathered the Shanghai God
before that economic journalist
overlooked the Q I made of myself.
On the green outside, *The Galway Hooker*
riffled with a squall off the Atlantic,
its sheet-steel rig heaving and quivering . . .
Somewhere a till gloated : *I Ching, I Ching*
like asdic basketing a submarine
then 'O.K.?' which was possibly 'O.Cé?'
asked the door of my palace of wisdom.
I brought up the Irish *abha* ('river'),
'ea', its lovely lost English sister,
name of Babylon's water deity,
then launched into my own flood-narrative.
The answer was Noah's, Utnapishtim's;
'Now tell me what you mean when you say "ark"?'.

B I Ballad

When He put a(n) *h* into Abraham
there wasn't a run on Dumbarton spam
but folk niggled when they should've begat –
say it this way you must, you must say that –

till all they could get up was objections.
Hence Tamar-Tephi's flight with Jacob's Stone,
your genuine Ark of the Covenant
and royal matchmakers to County Ant-

rim. Our Princess married an Irish king,
Elizabeth II descending;

the Ark stopped at Tara, the Stone took in
'Saint Colme's Inch', anchoring in London.

So there we are: not some wandering Jews
but British and Israelite and kosher;
His imperial tribe by Him chosen
to rule and stave off thin ends of wedges.

Cosby's Noah couldn't know 'a cubit':
our number's prime Egyptology mensch
proved The Great Pyramid of Giza built
'to the forerunner of the British inch.'

These inches, feet, measured Jerusalem
in His blue Jacobean English tongue:
bang on the M of the Millennium
we'll hear His trump and here we'll come again!

Traditional

My uncle measures me aged one:
'arse-high to a magpie's gallus-button!'

The day I married I watched two
threaten the stitching of their shiny suits

like the drunks at our wedding-dance.
I noticed the first time at my third glance

between the shoulders of those suits
a hint of a glint of gunmetal blue;

tails held with waiterly aplomb
splashing the colours of a petrol-bomb;

the mercury-tilt to their eyes.
Four of them mean birth. A dearth comes with five;

noisy families thick as thieves
augurs and understood relations have

by maggot-pies and choughs and rooks
the skewbald as familiar with six.

Seven babes buried in the dark.
Blood-libel birds, murderers from the ark.

Westminster Muse

Politicians have long recognised that a subtle use of poetic techniques is an essential part of their trade. Back to Basics is really about allit-eration: the superficial plausibility conferred by chiming consonants. John Major himself took a lurch into verse recently –

The rector spoke tonight in rhyme
And captivated us all the time.
It even made me forget
That he in times past
Once worked for the BBC.
That made him feel distinctly odd
But thankfully drove him back to God
So I thought I'd follow his lead and say
My message in the very same way.
My call tonight is clear and bright:
Don't worry boys, the country's alright.
Interest rates down and inflation low,
Exports up and we're ready to go.
Things are better and they won't get worse,
We can even expect the grace in verse.
So rector, into the pulpit and say:
God bless Britain we're on our way!

(28th Jan. 1994, Leeds Chamber of Commerce.)

– which prompted the Guardian to remark that we all know doggerel when we see it. If so, why are so many tongue-tied in the face of poetry? But our MPs are an exception. We sent 20 New Generation poems from the chosen books to many public figures in film, theatre, as well as politics. Most were too busy, but the MPs turned up trumps.

NEIL KINNOCK

Sometimes I think that, in the same way that only doctors sit on the General Medical Council, only poets should assess poets.

The subtle arts and sciences of poetry cannot properly be judged by those who have not had the courage to commit their lyrical thoughts and sombre dreams to print. And then I rouse myself and in-wardly declare 'I *know* what I like – and that will do for someone who reads quite a lot, understands some and digests a bit of poetry'. It's a view from the terraces ...

In this team of New Generation Poets, I can't reduce my forward line to less than five: Moniza Alvi's 'Dot in a Painting by Miro' is a delicate and whimsical expression of everyone's desire simulta-neously to be anonymous and distinctive. Simon

Armitage's 'And if it snows ...' is a simple, short evocative epitaph to a kindly, steady, sensible man who had warts of savagery and dishonesty. In 'Enclosed Wheatfield with Rising Sun', Pauline Stainer translates Van Gogh into words that do him justice – and then puts a memorable barb into the beauty. Lavinia Greenlaw's 'Science for Poets' in-triguingly transmits the sense of awe and hope that lay people feel when they realise that the painstak-ing, repetitive actions of scientists using measure-ments that go 'deep into decimal places' are the source of miracles. 'Fundamentals' by Ian Duhig has a muscular missionary taking the Bible and the 'bolt-action Martini-Henry' to heathen lands. It is pro-found and uproariously funny – a satire that carries messages for our age. I'll be using it in a Poems and Pints evening in South Wales in a few months time ... God willing.

KENNETH BAKER

The promotion of a group of younger poets could imply that there is a movement which marks some break with the recent past and which has some common thread or unifying purpose. I found it very interesting to read these poets for although there is nothing like a school or a cohesive group of poets – indeed individually all these poets would shun that – nonetheless there is a certain commonality.

First, they are all accessible. They are easy to read and few of the poems have to be read a second time in order to determine their meaning. There is virtu-ally no obscurity, no metaphysical contemplation, no surrealist abstraction and little sense of mystery. Rhyme forms tend to be conventional and they scan. This does not mean to say that the poems are dull and unoriginal, indeed many of them are fine.

Second, their subjects are rooted in the present – skinheads, playing pool, washing-up, clearing up snow, a Sony Walkman, Canary Wharf, and the horrors of a holiday in China wittily described by Kathleen Jamie. The poems, however, are not dull or mundane. I liked the sustained tension in Glyn Maxwell's 'Ginger, you're going to die' ('Song to the Skinhead'). Don Paterson's Guinness drinking pool-player triumphantly asserts that, 'I would screw back the globe, given somewhere to stand'. Some search for identity and association. I liked Elizabeth Garrett's 'The slipper wants a foot' ('In Absentia'). In her poem 'I would like to be a dot in a painting by Miro', Moniza Alvi writes:

The fact that I am not a perfect circle
Makes me more interesting in this world.
People will stare for ever.

Ian Duhig in a sharp political comment recreates an amusing speech of a missionary in Africa with the message backed up with 'a bolt action Martini-Henry'. Carol Ann Duffy has written a beautiful poem on prayer, 'Some nights, although we are faithless, the truth/ enters our hearts, that small familiar pain'. The phrase that stuck in my memory was from Jamie McKendrick's 'Windrose':

While a plinth of sunlight turned the sea's roof turquoise
And tides lashed the concrete calthrops of the breakwater.

This promotion will bring to a much wider audience some very good poetry by some fine poets. It does reveal the very high quality of poetry that is being written today.

DENIS HEALEY

The two poems which impressed me most are wholly different in tone, style and content. Michael Hofmann's 'From A to B and Back Again' is dry, colloquial and matter of fact, as he describes Barnet, his 'glottal stop' – a cross between Betjeman and Larkin. The central image of the Caesarean scars as a suburban railway track still lingers in my imagination.

Pauline Stainer's 'Enclosed Wheatfield with Rising Sun' explodes with expressionist violence like a poem by David Gascoyne – does anyone read him nowadays? It is a perfect re-creation of a Van Gogh, compared with which Hofmann's poem is a Lowry. At first I found the invocation of a nuclear explosion a little fictitious. After all, Robert Oppenheimer was deeply unhappy about his involvement with America's atomic programme. Now I feel it wholly appropriate. It extrapolates Van Gogh's images to a natural conclusion, as he himself did in his very late painting 'Cornfield with Crows'.

HARTLEY BOOTH

The New Generation Poets were a good read. Kathleen Jamie was authentic in China, though her title 'for lovers' would have been more aptly 'for tourists'. Don Paterson's realistic 'Ferryman's Arms' was evocative. Mick Imlah did not contest the Lord Chancellor's insomnia song in Iolanthe but it was a good topic. Moniza Alvi wanted to be a dot in a Miro painting and went for the deeply perceptive. Carol Ann Duffy and Ian Duhig chose Back to Basics. Elizabeth Garrett was groping for something special with 'the slipper wants a foot' ('In Absentia') and Lavinia Greenlaw was workmanlike in her excellent 'River History'.

In the end, I chose Sarah Maguire's 'Mushrooms à la Grecque'. She wrote an arresting poem about real life, a relationship and food. She began with a show-stopping: 'Halfway through the washing up' and continued with the wonderfully funny and mystifying verse:

All the places we made love
have been pulled down
or converted into something healthier

Was she referring to tents? Or the back of some flea pit Odeon cinema? We are left to wonder. Her topic 'stirred in the colon' and her poem stuck in the mind.

ROY HATTERSLEY

Poetry with a sting in its tail is not usually to my tastes, but Ian Duhig's 'Fundamentals' is wonderfully funny, and much is forgiven those who make us laugh. The poem appeals to all my prejudices – the missionary as salesman and the Bible as a justification to build an empire on which the sun never sets. I rarely enjoy 'Political poetry' but in 'Fundamentals' the attraction of the absurd Priest and the inherent absurdity of his sermon is irresistible.

I am not sure if 'when I say God is everywhere ... it is not because He is exceptionally fat' catches my imagination because the two concepts are so incongruous or because they have a crazy relationship which I cannot describe. 'My wife doesn't like it when you watch her go to the toilet' is certainly a valuable addition to the respectable catechism. 'Baptism starts at sundown' revives memories of the old joke about General Franco, the bishop, the battalion of Moorish irregulars and the hosepipe. Then at the end, there is the Martini-Henry – 'Naming of Parts', pickled in vinegar. I have learnt 'Fundamentals' by heart. I cannot imagine where I will recite it.

> *There are those who say that the two particular contributions this country has made to the civilisation of the world have been lyric poetry and political wisdom (and others say that they combine in cricket). As a journeyman politician I make no comment on the second; of the first I am wholly sure.*
>
> *Peter Brooke, Heritage Secretary*

ROBERT CRAWFORD
Talkies

ROBERT CRAWFORD WAS BORN IN 1959 IN BELLSHILL, NEAR GLASGOW. HE STUDIED AT THE UNIVERSITIES of Glasgow and Oxford, where he wrote a D. Phil.. thesis on Eliot, published as *The Savage and the City in the Work of T. S. Eliot*. He now teaches English at the University of St Andrews and edits the international poetry magazine, *Verse*. Crawford's first book was *A Scottish Assembly* (Chatto, 1990); *Talkies* (Chatto) followed in 1992.

Crawford is a prolific critic and an influential editor, as well as a poet. His energy and discrimination have made him a key figure in the Scottish poetry renaissance. He seems to be a happy man, straddling the academic/creative dichotomy with ease – in fact his work relishes all such interfaces. Crawford is a great internationalist, and is one of the few NG poets who *admits* to an interest in postmodernism: 'I do bounce it around quite a lot, like a tennis ball that's hard to control'. There is an excitement about Crawford's work – excitement about Scotland, science and technology, the plurality of things. Some of these come together in a poem like 'Iteration', which takes the notion of fractal patterns, endlessly proliferating on the computer, and extends this to life: 'another day of being in love –/One water droplet, then four, the singular/That is also plural'. 'Simultaneous Translation' cleverly pins down the dislocation of our times, call it postmodernism if you like: 'It fills up the pause when you finish speaking,/Or even before you've stopped,//Gets between the chewy biro and the word processor'. In 'Kypie' the faultline is a single vowel change: the Strathgowkies don't like the Strathgawkies, and vice versa. This is one of his most effective poems in Scots, hilarious but also menacing: ' Strathgawkers waant/ Total Strathgawkinization'. John Bayley has commented on the way that Crawford's 'clipped prose couplets and sentences rarely have anything spontaneous and melodic about them'. The poetry is in the exuberance, the cross-referencing, the juxtapositions of Scottish icons, acute textual awareness, and a fascination with the new Silicon Glen 'chip of a nation'. **(PF)**

Robert Crawford writes:
Directly or obliquely, a good poem is faithful to the language of its age. If it sounds unidiomatic, it sinks. At the same time, I love the idea of poems that incline towards another tongue. Unless equally fluent in English, Scots, and Gaelic, all Scots are aware of a language at once alien and familiar. I wanted some sense of that interplay and inclining of languages in *Talkies*, not just because it articulated something about Scotland, but because it articulated something about experience. We're always alive on the edge of the foreign translating each other and the world. A lot of my favourite poems – like Eliot's 'Marina' – seem to have an ear cocked, trying to tune in to a new and distant station.

I like funny poems too. What's more human than

a laugh? There has to be room for many different kinds of poetry – experimental, impure, straight-forward, compacted. Just as the range of genetic strains, of dialects, of language makes for a bubbling up of delight and variety, so all sorts of poetries purposefully co-exist. Often the most interesting poets are those using what's been sidelined, implicitly or explicitly branded 'unpoetic'.

Eliot I have admired since I first read him. He has the great gift of not repeating himself. I'd like my own books of poems to provide variety.

Three influential 20th C. books:
Hugh MacDiarmid, *Collected Poems*; Edwin Morgan, *Collected Poems*; Les Murray, *Collected Poems*.

THREE POEMS BY ROBERT CRAWFORD

The Numties

The parsnip Numties: I was a teenager then,
Collecting clip-together models
Of historical windsocks, dancing the Cumbernauld bump.

Satirical pornography, plant-staplers, nostalgiaform shoes
Were brochure-fresh. It was numty-four
I first saw a neighbour laughing in a herbal shirt.

Moshtensky, Garvin, Manda Sharry —
Names as quintessentially Numties
As Hearers and Bonders, duckponding, or getting a job

In eradication. Everything so familiar and sandwiched
Between the pre-Numties and the debouche of decades after.
I keep plunging down to the wreck

Of the submerged Numties, every year
Bringing back something jubilantly pristine,
Deeper drowned, clutching my breath.

Scotch Broth

A soup so thick you could shake its hand
And stroll with it before dinner.

The face rising to its surface,
A rayfish waiting to be stroked,

Is the pustular, eat-me face of a crofter,
Turnipocephalic, white-haired.

Accepting all comers, it's still our nation's
Flagsoup, sip-soup; sip, sip, sip

At this other scotch made with mutton
That intoxicates only

With peas and potatoes, chewy uists of meat.
All races breath over our bowl,

Inhaling Inverness and Rutherglen,
Waiting for a big teuchtery face

To compose itself from carrots and barley
Rising up towards the spoon.

Unstinting

Dawn's fractured bone
Windchills your channels,

Small, remote radio stations
Broadcasting Christ to the waves.

The held note's
Hearing-aid whine draws congregations

Aboard ferries and over causeways.
Steelworks are swimming through the oceans,

Dirtying them as they migrate.
Dying patients, the newborn in incubators

Each have their own long, caring numbers,
Tags on the red legs of birds.

                    *

If a nuclear sub's
Viking blush passes down the islands,

Embarrassing Harris, North Uist, Benbecula,
Humiliating their stones,

I will mount a search. I will put to sea
Towards the shepherd's crook of psalms,

Community's tough-minded holy grit
Round which an incarnate pearl

Shines across so-called Dark Ages
Its sol-fa brecbennach of calm.

Bakhtin Basics

by Ian Gregson

Robert Crawford,
Identifying Poets: Self and Territory in
Twentieth Century Poetry,
Edinburgh University Press, £25.00,
ISBN 0 7486 0409 X

Robert Crawford's passionate concern in his latest critical book is to defend what he calls 'the poetry of home' against those who would dismiss it as merely regionalist. What makes this defence effective is the way he links it to the thinking about identity in the writings of Mikhail Bakhtin, who regards it as always and everywhere hybrid and shifting. So he quotes the Russian theorist – whose work has acquired, over the past decade, such posthumous importance – saying that the 'realm of culture has no internal territory: it is entirely distributed along the boundaries, boudaries pass everywhere, through its every aspect'.

This means that, for the poetry of home, the importance of elsewhere is as pressing as that of here. Too much focus on a writer's own tradition leads to an essentialist belief in 'some sort of unaltering Scotland or Wales or Canada' and Crawford opposes this with a Bakhtinian stress on interaction with significant others which exist inside as well as outside each culture. He's especially acute when describing the collision of self and other in the work of Scottish poets like Hugh MacDiarmid, Sorley Maclean, Frank Kuppner and W.N. Herbert, and revealing how 'the poet who writes in Scots in Scotland is likely to have to engage with the "other" of English; equally the poet who writes in English in Scotland is likely to be subtly aware of Gaelic and Scots identities which are Scots also'. But what he says about his own countrymen has also a representative significance for all poets and the way they identify themselves by simultaneously identifying with their own cultures and engaging with non-native traditions: 'Identity for the Scottish identifying poets, and for identifying poets generally, is not a matter of purity but of an amalgam of resources'.

However, Crawford uses Bakhtin too loosely at times and the strain shows especially when he deals with non-Scottish poets. To apply the crucial Bakhtinian concept of the 'dialogic' to John Ashbery is to forget that Bakhtin's own most important dialogue was with Marxism, and that while the dialogic emphasizes plurality it is also premised upon a belief in the reality of social experience. Crawford himself seems to be aware of this when he refers in his 'Introduction' to Bakhtin's eagerness 'to see language and writing as grounded in the actual'. The cogency of this realist side in Bakhtin arises from the way it gives something for his equally important polyphonic emphasis to brace itself against. But his greatest usefulness for the understanding of contemporary poetry lies precisely in the way he takes plurality and the actual with equal seriousness. It's crucial, then, to differentiate between the way that the dialogic dwells on the lived experience of each differing voice and the way that Ashbery's extreme anti-realism invokes a frictionless vista of multiplying perspectives that endlessly cancel each other out. For, as Crawford says, Ashbery's work 'gives the impression of being generated by virtually a blank, a nobody, a rather sad speaker whose very existence may be called into question as pronouns flicker and merge'.

It's distressing to see the dialogic which, in its subtle formulation by Bakhtin, manages to be both subversive and politically responsible, both fabulatory and committed, used to defend a poetic which is ultimately so conservative. But at least Ashbery is fun to read. I found it even stranger that Crawford could invoke Bakhtin in order to praise that overrated reactionary Les Murray, whose arguments are not with others but with himself and the sacred land. Murray is only accidentally dialogic – the real thrust of his work is in the opposite direction, involving a Nature/Mind dialectic, a Romantic retread version of the monologic search for a transcendant synthesis. This leads to a privileging of the 'natural' over the social and consequently to some highly repressive political attitudes.

This is unfortunate but if it starts a debate which reveals the genuine usefulness of Bakhtin for the understanding of contemporary poetry its outcome will be wholly positive. This would involve the dialogic being thoroughly dissociated from both Ashbery and Murray – mostly opposites except in their conservatism – and relevantly applied to poets like Carol Ann Duffy, Douglas Dunn and Paul Muldoon whose work negotiates between postmodernism and realism, and invokes jarring perspectives but insists on the lived experiences from which they arise.

ELIZABETH GARRETT
The Rule of Three

ELIZABETH GARRETT WAS BORN IN LONDON IN 1958 AND MOVED TO THE CHANNEL ISLANDS AT THE age of one. Her father is half French, and France and French poetry has always been important to her. She read English and French at York University and has written an Oxford D.Phil thesis on the fool in contemporary poetry. She now works for the Voltaire Foundation in Oxford. She was one of *Poetry Review*'s New British Poets in the Winter 1987 issue. Her pamphlet *The Mortal Light* was published by the Mandeville Press in 1990. *The Rule of Three* was published by Bloodaxe in 1991 and reviewed by Helen Dunmore in *Poetry Review*, Spring 1992.

Elizabeth Garrett has mostly remained aloof from the currents of contemporary poetry. During the '80s most of her poems appeared by choice in only two magazine, *Poetry Review* and *South West Review*. She did, though, imbibe contemporary influences at the Old Fire Station poetry workshop in Oxford, 1982-5. Her musical training, painter's eye and grounding in Gravesian lyricism have produced as near to a pure lyric poet as we'll get in our times. Her subjects are womanhood, love, nature. The poems in *The Rule of Three* were written over a ten-year period and the long sequence 'Rumaucourt' (1982) does betray that period's penchant for lush and precise imagery ('The table charts/ an archipelago/ Of wine stains. Coral atolls, skerries, scars/ Of civilisation in the woodgrain sea').

Besides creating gorgeous consonantal music like 'where crests of lilac break/ To foam; and in their leaves, the soft/ Lallation of the waves' ('Nilak'), her work often has a stark, impassioned note: 'In Absentia' is one of the strongest love poems of recent years, absence causing the mind to wallow drunkenly: 'See what the mind has done, has left undone –'Ah, calves knees thighs, and the night comes./ It is no good; I get no further than the ground on which you stood./ The slipper wants a foot'. **(PF)**

Elizabeth Garrett writes:
I intended to pursue a career in music. At 16, I left my Channel Island home to further a musical training at Wells Cathedral School. An unanalytical love of the sensual and musical properties of language developed here into a need to explore and understand the way meaning is manipulated by form. Poetry became the natural object – and eventually expression – of this desire. I think with my tongue. The properties of the sheer *sensual* in words – whatever the language – fascinates me: the way they feel on the tongue; how they strike the ear; their shape on the page and in the mind's eye; their weight and density. Word-play is one of the antechambers of poetry. But so, too, is silence. I think my best work manages to listen to the silence from

which it has emerged. Poetry must haunt, which is not a question of mere memorability, but something to do with the undertow beneath the surface of word-sound and word-sense. The rhythmic tension of a poem, its cadences, and the hidden persuaders of form are a crucial part of this capacity to haunt. If an image strikes, it must also go on resounding.

Three influential 20th C. books:
Robert Graves, *Poems*, selected by himself; John Berryman, *The Dream Songs*; I have to struggle to name a third, the more pronounced influences (especially John Donne) belonging not to the twentieth century.

THREE POEMS BY ELIZABETH GARRETT

Testament
(For Katie)

Because she was so small and our names
Had tied a knot in her clenched fist;
Because the script said she was my sister
And I the elder, I let her come.
How neat the excuses of reason.

It was a green hour, and the sap waxing.
The house was overgrown, void of all reason:
Out of the windows skimmed
Whole creamy plates of elderflower
That did not shatter, crumbling
Inaudibly in the wind;
Mice nested in the memory of the floor.
It was a green season, and the sap rising.

She was light as a scrap of litmus and possessed
Between the red blood flushed with pumping
And the bruised violet
All the spectrum of desire. I would test
Her for the alkalinity of my lust.
To myself I said, 'Not the dream that violates,
But the script – its cues and promptings
Even the illiterate can't resist'.

So we were pulled down, blundering with the sun
That burst through bushes
Banging our eyes with its blindness.
Then I smelt salt. It was like one colour
Bleeding into another – so clear
I could distinguish the brine from the fresh.
All this by a breath indrawn
At the rivermouth where the sea thrust its tongue.

Oh I knew the place: the waves' cross-rhythms
I was reared on, the fretted reef, the lure
Of undertow and the foam like elderflowers
Dissolving. I waded to the limit of a world
Where the pure and the salt wrestled,
My hands and my tongue tied, growing numb
Below the knees, and the stumbling child –
Before me – going down.

The Phrygian Mode

They will say we stole it; like the sweet
Music laced with Athene's breath
That Marsyas wooed, even to his death –
A stripped reed, a stopped flute.

Put your mouth to my mouth, but do not kiss:
Say the gods are kind, say they are not jealous.
So, we shall sing when the future flays
Our shadows from us and the hoar frost
Blossoms in the wound. What is Marsyas
And the blood's cry curdling on the breath
But a figure of speech, an old myth?

Put your lips to my lips: it is no fault
Our two souls mingle in the one breath,
Since the gods will judge, and even death
Steals music from the bone's flute.

Imago

When I returned
You had the stillness of the garden
On you. No-one called,
You said, but silence –
Though the bees passed through like merchants
With their sacks of gold.

I believed;
And felt that distance spread, then close
Between us, as the hinged
Leaves of butterflies –
Love to love's own blind image
So trustingly inclines.

Hours later,
With a lepidopterist's cool passion
You recalled the one visit:
How, when the Painted Lady
Settled on your heart, her thorax thrilled
With the listening of it.

MICHAEL HOFMANN
Corona, Corona

MICHAEL HOFMANN WAS BORN IN FREIBURG, GERMANY IN 1957 TO GERMAN PARENTS (HIS FATHER was Gert Hofmann, the novelist). His parents brought him to England in 1961. He was educated at Cambridge University and now works as a freelance writer, reviewer and translator. His three books for Faber are *Nights in the Iron Hotel* (1984), *Acrimony* (1986), and *Corona, Corona* (1993). He won a Cholmondley Award in 1984 and the Geoffrey Faber Memorial Prize in 1988.

Michael Hofmann is one of the few New Generation poets with a highly developed interest in the traditional poetic technique of phrase-making. Throughout his work there are laconic thumbnail formulations, part nervous tic, part sympathetic magic, which at their best are unforgettable mantras: the quatrain poem 'Sally' for instance: 'A blue button-through day, a pink, a black,/the little black dress, the bricks circulating /through the central heating system,/ sorrow, lust and peristalsis at three'. He likes to encapsulate worlds in triads - 'dancing, miscegenation and cigars ', 'blatant, ravenous, post-coital', 'asleep, motorized, tidal' – and his syllepsis is the best in the business: 'wearing a pleasant frown and predistressed denims', 'an electric grille and a siege mentality'.

Like Hugo Williams, Hofmann has written much about his father, a sacred monster who has cast a huge shadow over Hofmann's life. His sense of apartness, being German and having to engineer his English identity, have provided the emotional force behind his poems. Hofmann's descriptive gifts and cultural range have never been in doubt but his habit of undercutting himself, throwing away his lines ('as though I'd spoken in asides for twenty five years') has bothered some critics. In his recent work, though (see 'From A to B and Back Again', page 49), the blend of knowingness and innocence is wholly successful - he is not afraid of words like 'cicatrice' and 'analphabete', nor of invoking 'my brave love'. Hofmann's poetry is an acquired taste worth acquiring. **(PF)**

Michael Hofmann writes:
I started writing when I was 19, and now, almost twice that, I hold pretty much the opposite ideas (although in other ways, not much has changed). I wrote down Poe's phrase, 'a frictionless expressive purity ', eschewed sound, repetition, pleasingness, stanza breaks, wrote poems the size and shape and texture of bricks, but that still had a certain cunning.

Since then I have gotten interested in the chemistry or alchemy of word combinations – impurity or friction in Poe's formula,

'logopoiea' in Pound's. I have as a touchstone the first words of a Robert Lowell poem, 'Pale ale, molar drain', a line of Les Murray's, 'In 1980, in a street of Federation houses', or even, God forgive me, my own 'A blue button-through day, a pink, a black'.

These things are supposed not to let the reader go. I believe, with Gottfried Benn, that, 'the ability to write fascinatingly is a primary one', and that nothing else ('polystrophic rhymed addresses to loved ones and aunts') is worth shit. That what matters in writing has not been codified: it has to make you freeze and burn, or take the top of your head off, as Emily Dickinson said.

I write about myself, but not out of solipsism. If I had somewhere to stand I would write about the world. I like a kind of humour where no one quite dares to laugh.

Three influential 20th C. books:
Rainer Maria Rilke, *Neue Gedichte* (1907); Robert Lowell, *Life Studies* (1959); Joseph Brodsky, *A Part of Speech* (1980).

THREE POEMS BY MICHAEL HOFMANN

From A to B and Back Again

The Northern Line had come out into the open,
was leaving tracks like a curving cicatrice.
There was Barnet, my glottal stop, trying hard
to live up to its name, colloquial and harmless and trite.

The place was sunny and congested, brick and green trim,
it had the one-of-everything-and-two-butchers
of a provincial town. First, I dropped into
the maternity hospital by mistake . . .

The porter was an analphabete, but together
we found your name, down among the Os,
and there you were, my brave love,
in a loose hospital gown that covered nothing;

pale; on an empty drip; and eager to show me
your scars, a couple of tidy crosses
like grappling hooks, one in the metropolis,
the other some distance away, in the unconcerned suburbs.

Reprinted, with permission, from *Corona, Corona* (Faber, 1993)

The Station Road, The Primrose Path

To the station in my red boots in the mid '80s:
to London, a broken-off book review in my pocket –
in this, as in everything else (the station,
the boots, the mid '80s) a generation late.

Meeting you coming the other way, all of a sudden
I urgently wanted to proceed no further
than the back of the nearest bicycle shed
and there go to ground like two snails . . .

No to cerebration, no to the Spillers building
and the cachet of phoney language schools,
no to the delayed electrification of the East Coast Line
and my unwritten, never-to-be-written style paragraph.

Conversation

'Too drunk to fuck or drive, the baby with its father,
my doubles brought out in two tot glasses,
some herby German swill, sweet, I like it, *digestif*, he says,

I'm drunk, I have my foot on the chair, my knee
up alongside my face, I haven't eaten for two days,
he's thinking about my legs, I tell him I'm drunk,

America is a cesspool, I blame television,
then I all but empty my pack of Camels into my glass,
he takes a wet cigarette and lights it from my lighter,

I knock over my second tot glass and it puddles on the table,
he's talking but I can't understand the half of it,
though he has a poem that has "forever England" in it,

and I tell him I like that, well, it's probably enough anyway,
then I suddenly feel very quiet, he's asking me
about my writing and I lean forward and puke.'

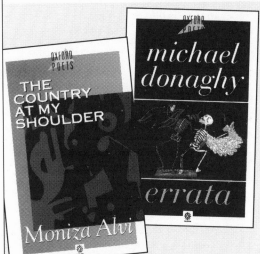

Lvov Poems
by Michael Hofmann

Zbigniew Herbert,
Mr Cogito,
Trans. John Carpenter and
Bogdana Carpenter,
OUP, £7.99, ISBN 0 19 282873 8
Adam Zagajewski,
Canvas,
Trans. Renata Gorczynski, Benjamin Ivry
and C.K. Williams
Faber, 5.99, ISBN 0 571 16906 6

Given that he has had the same publisher for years, OUP in England and Ecco in America, the same fine and devoted translators, John and Bogdana Carpenter, and that, in my opinion, he would not have been greatly exalted by receiving the Nobel Prize at any time in the last 25 years, I can only conclude that there is some unfortunate obstruction (paper rationing?!) or else that Zbigniew Herbert is bafflingly badly published in English: so little of his work has appeared, at such long intervals, and out of order.

This book, *Mr Cogito*, contains work from 1969 to 1974; other Cogito poems have appeared not as the jacket says in his *Selected Poems*, but in his other book, *Report from the Beseiged City*. They have been around in German for at least 20 years: at some point translations can no longer be referred to as 'long awaited', they are shamefully delayed. And yet, in the midst of all this muddle and inertia, the author's photograph is changing, the boyish, puckish Herbert, a cherub with horns, has been replaced by a tense, lined, almost burnt-looking senatorial figure, his fingers clamping a frightened smile in place, and his hair, like 'the hair of the tree to which Marsyas was fastened/is white/completely'. Herbert is 70 this year: he will not be around for ever.

I have two things to say about *Mr Cogito*: one, that it is not Herbert at his best, the other, that Herbert is Herbert. There are only a handful of poems that approach the epochal excellence of 'Elegy of Fortinbras' and many of the pieces in *Report from the Beseiged City*: 'Sequoia', 'Caligula', 'Mr Cogito and Pure Thought', 'Mr Cogito Tells about the Temptation of Spinoza', and the first and last poems in the book, 'Mr Cogito Looks at His Face in the Mirror' and 'The Envoy of Mr Cogito'. The first (reminding me of

the fool who praised Tom Paulin's first book for looking at things other than his own face in the mirror – as if a poem was only ever one thing, or a subject defined what could be said about it) accommodates thousands of years of civilized and uncivilized history. It is a rare example in this book of Herbert's wonderful historical agility, classic *multum in parvo*: 'ears protruding too far two shells of skin/ probably a legacy from the ancestor who caught the echo/of a rumbling procession of mammoths over the steppe'. He is a poet for whom time is an open lift, where he goes up and down at will, and who can similarly compress or expand space: 'beautiful as a cathedral of fern preserved in coal', 'a rose picked at dawn sheds petals in panic/by evening it is only a burnt grove of stamens'. These transformations are proof of an epic imagination. The examples came from *Report from the Beseiged City*: he doesn't do it much in the new book.

Mr Cogito – like the series habit or the growing of side whiskers, according to P.G. Wodehouse – is the kind of thing poets of a certain age adopt. He is Herbert out of armour, demilitarized, a kind of soft shelled figure. For all his cultivated austerity – 'I thump on the board/and it prompts me/with the moralist's dry poem/yes – yes/no – no' in the early poem, 'A Knocker' – Herbert is a lovely and abashed sensualist. Ironically and typically, this comes out much more in his prose, like last year's *Still Life with Bridle* (Cape), with its amorous descriptions of 17th century Dutch genre paintings, and the stolid bourgeois culture that made them possible. When this quality emerges in the poems, it is accompanied by a delicate squirming on the part of the poet:

> to tell the truth Mr Cogito
> is not completely without fault
> he was unable to detach
> his inner eye
> from the mailbox
> the smell of the sea was in his nostrils
> crickets tickled his ear
> and he felt her absent fingers under his ribs.

Talk about Herbert – Alvarez certainly, the Carpenters, even Heaney – concentrates almost exclusively on his civic and political virtues. But even to say, as Heaney says on the cover, 'This poetry is far more than "dissident"', is to say dismayingly little. We in the West could not honestly claim to be able to read him like that, not then, still less now. It is time for Herbert to be read by formalists: by people who notice and take pleasure in his unpunctuated sentences, trip along his unsignposted and surprising pathways to some final vista, caress the Möbius twists of his thought and imagery.

Adam Zagajewski, born in 1945 and like Herbert in Lvov, is the pre-eminent poet in the generation after Herbert's. I adored his *Tremor* when it came out: the lushness of his comma'ed catalogues (so different from Herbert), cadences not of sound because they weren't the original words, but of sense, of things:

> Lances, banners, sabers, horses.
> Horses, razors, alphabet blocks,
> warm green lamps, women, manners, burning
> conversations, and the yellow ashes of the
>   books.
> A real lady prays only in French.
> Over an étagère, a swarthy Tatar Madonna,
> immobile, like a hummingbird.
> A huge family reunion. The children are sent
> to the garden. Vodka bitter as wormwood
> and the Old Testament of jokes.
>   ('A Polish Dictionary')

Perhaps Renata Gorczynski (his translator) didn't have a good sense of what a poem in English ought to sound like, or perhaps she overrode it, but the results were wonderful line-breaks and a refreshingly abrupt idiom. It is good to read 'groans and moans' once in a while, and if that seems a picayune point (like Herbert's absence of full stops) try and imagine *A Hundred Years of Solitude* in standard English.

In *Canvas*, Gorczynski is joined by C.K. Williams (a friend and neighbour of Zagajewski in Paris) who certainly does know about the sound of poems in English; but in another way it seems an odd pairing, Zagajewski with his fugitive, scrappy, beautiful, Klee-like poems, and Williams, conscience-driven, upright, without compression, worrying away at old trauma. I don't know if it's the translation or not, but I like *Canvas* less than the first book. There is a sense of more polish than Polish now, a sense of words deliberated over, an occasional sense of effort to keep the poem-ship on an even keel. I don't like 'lambent', or 'author' as a verb. A line like 'A surveyor-raven methodically measures a field' effortlessly passes muster as a cleverly sounding English line: I would have wished it more rickety and careless, as *Tremor* sounded to me.

Undeniably, though, Zagajewski's poems have also changed – somewhat. They seem to me more ordered (there is a sonnet, but that's not what I mean), more controlled, less wild, more upturned to praise and to hope. If the first book was like a sonata, one pert and affectionate voice, one rapid, acquisitive, sometimes tear-filled regard, there is more

orchestra in *Canvas*. Also, there is no longer the complete absence of any acknowledgement for the occasion of the poems – which was such an amazing feature of *Tremor*. Here, there are elegies, love poems, political poems, all pretty explicit – eg, 'Watching *Shoah* in a Hotel Room in America'. Of course, also the quirks of the voice (he uses adverbs beautifully, the way a bad novelist might) are no longer new.

But I don't want to overdo my dissatisfaction. *Canvas* is a good book by a wonderful and idiosyncratic poet. Zagajewski still has his habits, ideas still float along on winds of things, he is still as compendious and constituted as a child's encyclopedia, he still writes with manifest and contagious delight of the pleasures and opulence of existence:

> Birdsong diminishes.
> The moon sits for a photo.
> The wet cheeks of streets gleam.
> Wind brings the scent of ripe fields.
> High overhead a small plane cavorts like a
>   dolphin.
>   ('A History of Solitude')

I don't know that anyone has written about this since the Imagists or early Stevens.

How We Made New Gen

New Generation Poets was conceived in an informal discussion between three publisher's editors at the National Poetry Competition prizegiving event in January 1993. They were Bill Swainson (Harvill), Christopher Reid (Faber) and Robin Robertson (then Secker, soon to be Cape). They felt that the strength of the new generation of poets justified a major celebration. They put the idea on hold while they published their spring lists and in May '93 took the idea to the Poetry Society, the Arts Council, the other publishers, and Waterstone's booksellers. A committee of these organizations was formed to select a panel of judges, appoint a publicist, raise funds from scratch, and appoint a Steering group ...

The New Gen Steering group comprised: Bill Swainson (Chair and prime mover), Gail Lynch (Colman Getty Publicity), Iain Stewart (Arts Council), Jacky Simms (Poetry Editor at OUP), Roger Bratchell (Waterstone's Marketing Manager), the Director of the Poetry Society (Chris Green and later Chris Meade), Peter Forbes (*Poetry Review*), Alex Zeman (Poetry Society Events), Morag McRae (Poetry Society Administration).

The timescale was very short to raise the necessary funds but the organizations listed on page 1 responded quickly and by August we knew that the promotion was viable. An important factor at this stage was the eagerness of many bodies to be associated with the promotion. The Arts Council were already involved in developing a project to broadcast poems in a new format on Radio. It was quickly realised that this project would benefit from the impetus of the New Generation, and Radio 1 FM expressed a strong wish to be associated with the promotion. As far as the media were concerned, Poems on Radio 1 was the principal novelty of the campaign, feeding into the search for 'the new rock 'n roll'.

The judges were working on the 120-odd books submitted throughout October and November. They

Michael Longley writes on being a New Generation judge

Over lunch about a year ago I felt privileged listening to Bill Swainson and Robin Robertson as they enthused about new poetry, first novels, collections of short stories by little-known writers. The publication of a first collection should be an unforgettable excitement for its author. For such editors the event seems to carry a comparable charge. In order to bring **NGP** into being, they joined forces with **Christopher Reid**, who has opened up the **Faber** list. The detailing and vision of **NGP** owes much to its three progenitors, especially **Bill Swainson**.

As one of the judges I am very proud of our roll-call of twenty. I wish them good poems and good days. The publicity has so far played down what I enjoy most in many of the poets: tense formality, learned knottiness, abstruse vocabularies, strange noises. I'm not sure that I want poetry to be the new rock 'n roll. Rock 'n roll took out of jazz the insistent beat and left the poetry behind. If I'm wrong, then I'm Gary Glitter.

assembled at the Poetry Society, under Melvyn Bragg's chairmanship, on December 8th to make their list of 20 poets. The list was announced to the press on January 12th. The timing, it should be explained, was a necessary consequence of the need to alert the book trade, to prepare the leaflets, posters and other publicity material, and to book the events.

The media coverage on January 13th was astonishing. Clearly some sort of chord had been touched (for a blow-by-blow account of this time, see Don Paterson's Diary on page 58). Since then, the poets have been assigned to their readings (see listings, p. 115), poems have appeared weekly in the *Observer*, and media coverage for May has been planned. The trickiest aspect of all has been poems on Radio 1. Clearly, bridging the gap between the high-energy delivery of what was once a 'more music' radio station and the more measured voices of poetry was a major challenge. At the time of writing, the tapes are in production (one-third of the 40 poems will be by New Generation poets, one third by other contemporary poets, one third celebrities reading classic poems). Given the intense spotlight directed on Radio 1 recently, these poems will be more eagerly awaited than any in history, if only because many people are sure it won't work. Tune in and see. Which applies to the whole project.

Rules of the Game

To qualify for selection, publishers were asked to submit collections by poets who would be under 40 at 30 April 1994 or who had been published for the first time since 1989. A collection was taken to mean a book of more than 32 pages with a spine. Poets had to be UK citizens or normally resident in the UK and their work had to be written in the English language. Publishers were only allowed one book per poet but could decide which that book should be. The publisher agreed to pay £500 towards the cost of the promotion for each poet finally selected.

The Judges

Melvyn Bragg – non-voting Chairman. Writer and broadcaster. Presents *The South Bank Show* **on LWT and** *Start the Week* **on BBC Radio 4.**
Margaret Busby – publisher and author. Most recently she edited *Daughters of Africa* **(Cape/Vintage).**
Vicki Feaver – poet. Her first collection was *Close Relatives* **(Secker & Warburg). Her new collection,** *The Handless Maiden,* **was one of the Cape poetry relaunch titles in April this year.**
Michael Longley – poet. He won the Whitbread Poetry Award for *Gorse Fires* **(Secker & Warburg, 1991).** *Poems:1963-1983* **is published by Penguin. Lives in Belfast.**
John Osborne – Professor of American Studies at Hull University and Editor of the poetry magazine *Bête Noire.*
James Wood – Chief Literary Critic of the *Guardian.*

Some of the New Gen team after the judging at the Poetry Society , 8 December, 1993. (l-r) back: Gail Lynch, Peter Forbes, Margaret Busby, Melvyn Bragg, Vicki Feaver, Michael Longley, John Osborne, Alex Zeman, Bill Swainson; front: Jacky Simms, Morag McRae, James Wood.

JAMIE McKENDRICK
The Kiosk on the Brink

JAMIE McKENDRICK WAS BORN IN LIVERPOOL AND HAS LIVED IN YORK, LIVERPOOL AND NOTTINGHAM. He has taught at the University of Salerno, Italy. He now lives in Oxford where he teaches part-time. His first collection, *The Sirocco Room,* was published by Oxford Poets in 1991. *The Kiosk on the Brink* (Oxford Poets, 1993) is reviewed on page 57.

Italian poetry has been vitally important to McKendrick: many of his poems are set in Italy and Montale is a pervasive influence. McKendrick is in thrall to the verbal glamour of decay: his poems are full of battered cars, rotting cuttlefish, and 'the Cement Factory's toxic plume'. 'De-Signifiers' in *The Sirocco Room* celebrates the microbes and insects that destroy texts. The effect, as in Montale, is the redemption of the fallen world through language. Rhythmically, this rich material is deftly marshalled: the pace is restrained but he has some fine endings – the wind ravaging a spider's web, 'snicking the links with its casual shears' (the links being also the web of life threatened by global warming); 'around which once the leaf-green planet turned', in a poem about his old car as a force of nature.

Personally, McKendrick's work is shot through with apprehension. Things are always hanging on threads – 'the intimate thread may fray like saliva / in a backdraught or seawind'. The brink of the book's title is a volcano and this stands as an emblem of other threatening forces. Tom Paulin, reviewing his first book, referred to his 'strangely laid-back despair'. Although he rarely writes personally in *The Kiosk on the Brink*, the bleak 'Home Thoughts', about postcards from a former lover, catches that note: 'the last things / you mention are the Parsee towers of silence / where the dead are left for vultures to attend./I warm to that. It sort of brings things home'. McKendrick has not received as much attention as some of the New Generation, but he's created poetry with a genuine Italian luxurance in that relatively stony place: the English language. **(PF)**

Jamie McKendrick writes:

The Navajo rugmakers learnt their craft, according to legend, from Spider Woman who taught them to break the pattern so as to leave a spirit outlet – the spirit being trapped by too much symmetry.

I'm drawn to the aesthetic behind this idea of irregularity – moments where the pattern of the poem breaks and opens onto the world. Though without the initial pattern, whether rhythmic or conceptual, you'd only have the confusion it's the poem's job to break free of.

If this sounds too much like escapology, I take heart from a passage in early Montale where he looks for the link that doesn't hold (*'l'anello che non tiene'*), the mistake in nature that might put us in the midst of a truth. The hope that the poem will offer something which isn't merely prefabricated or deterministic, and the pleasure that comes from being neither.

Three influential 20th C. books:

Elizabeth Bishop, *Geography III,* Eugenio Montale, *Ossi di sepia* (Cuttlefish Bones); Seamus Heaney, *Field Work.*

THREE POEMS BY JAMIE MCKENDRICK

Paestum

The three temples are like things with roots
that channel the weather into bedrock
and pulse with a low frequency way under earshot
earth rumours back into the stratosphere.

The uttermost limit of the Grand Tour,
its point of exhaustion and refreshment,
the travertine stonework rises like a
shimmering wall of sea although the sea

and its god have withdrawn from sight behind
the polished cubits of the perimeter wall
leaving the harbour stranded. Malaria
filled the spaces where the sea had been,

and shifting trade-routes and the tilt of power
and a black rain of lapilli
left this stone unroofed and tenantless, the haunt
by day of jackdaws and by night of owls.

Snakes that pose under the famous roses
at the edge of wedding photos last year claimed
a satin bride for Dis. The Doric columns
tower in TV adverts and tourist brochures

while the triglyphs still grip the entablature
like talons. On the diver's tomb in the museum
earth swells and might as well be water under
the silent leap of the diver

– his body finding itself in mid-flight
suddenly supple again and childlike, arched,
his weight assumed by air which any moment might
spring wide like the Sea Gate onto a burning source.

Span

Eye-level with the alps of ash and slag
I trawl my floor for a BT counterfoil
deep into its scarlet monitory phase
through shards and rags and scraps
and crizzled gold tobacco threads and these
long white hairs which must be mine

alas as no-one else
would venture into this rented room
except one short-haired black-haired cat.
And here's a flea he carried on his back,
a tiny emissary from the caliphat
of bad dreams, doing vaults and back-flips
onto three golden dusters, bought last year
and still sealed in polythene,
their hems blanket-stitched with crimson thread
in a series of small 'v's overlapping
the dictionary. Crimson: it burns a fuse
the length of a dusty trail of roots
back to Arabic: qirmizi:
meaning the Scarlet Grain insect which breeds
on the kermes oak – stuff Solomon hung
beneath the wrought-gold
five-cubit wingspan of the cherubim,
crimson lights up back along the line of
the trade-routes west, at each camel-stop
or port – a vowel-shift, a letter
dislodged from the throat to the palate
colouring the sound. My eyes lift
to the level of the window, facing east
onto brickwork, tarmac and slate tiles.
Upon the window-sill – a fly's black torso,
deep in the mire of last year's dust,
with its seraph wings still poised for flight
but cumbersome like panes
of leaded glass or paddles of cracked quartz,
tired for a while of beating at the air.

Windrose

When we threw caution to the winds, the city
was the city of winds which blew from the four points, the eight quarters
of the windrose, a star which creaked and skittered on its hinge
and reared dustdevils – helices, rootless, footloose, almost human –

and a palm frond swept the public garden paths
like a bird feigning lameness – shuffle, hop, another shuffle –
while a plinth of sunlight turned the sea's roof turquoise
and tides lashed the concrete calthrops of the breakwater.

On a calm day once from Posillipo I saw
the sea, way out, extrude a pillar of salt, a corkscrew
that tapped the deep and lifted shoals to rain down on our roofs
like wingless birds who'd flown through sheer assumption.

Reprinted from *The Kiosk on the Brink* by permission of Oxford Poets.

Seismic Survey

Roger Garfitt on the volcanic nuances of Jamie McKendrick

Jamie McKendrick,
The Kiosk on the Brink,
Oxford Poets, £6.99,
ISBN 0 19 283118 6

The *Kiosk* is poised *on the Brink* of a volcano – and so, in a sense, is the whole book, suggestively poised over images of social breakdown and imaginative risk. The real place 'Under the Volcano' where addicts shoot up 'between the Devil's Viaduct and the deep blue sea' elides into the inevitable place from which poetry comes. McKendrick gives his Italian and Sicilian landscapes a kind of magic realism ('lengths of air' is like a Garcia Marquez story in miniature) so that they become emblematic of the human condition, neither more nor less real than the plainly fabulous landscape of 'The Crystal Sky' where

> I lived in an outcrop of thinnest glass,
> a little showcase of bad habits
> – unspeakable things I did at night
>
> waiting for the Reprisal, the moon aqueous,
> rose-coloured, almost within reach.

The result is an unusually unified collection in which each poem informs the other and every one seems to stand for more than itself. Images of shock abound, not just the earth tremors of the volcano, 'a faint premonitory sprinkling of stones', or the sky tremors of 'the windrose, a star which creaked and skittered on its hinge', but the slow waves of shock after a car crash – 'if the earth might please/stop shaking up and down, the fields/kinking in small ashen troughs and crests', or a pervasive sense of 'Loss':

> If what you hear is like a field
> and the height of a lark above it
> then the field has dwindled and the wind
> bells on the razor wire around
> the verge ...

The earth never has stopped shaking. It remains permanently kinked and ashen. McKendrick's landscape is on 'The Wrong Side' of the tracks, a place where 'Goats chewed the shadows of the rock and gazed/ with proprietorial sarcasm' and 'a palm tree up to its chin / in white dust' mirrors us, 'stuck in this nothing ... up to our necks'. It's his version of Greeneland and already, after only two books, he can evoke it just by the weight of a phrase. His characteristic repetition, an echo that acts like an internal rhyme, 'within a footstep of the doorstep', 'rootless, footloose, almost human', 'a valley of shadows. / The shadow of her breasts', locks us formally into the impasse.

And yet someone shows up who has at least two of the characteristics of the Muse: she's 'Too good to be true (neither her strong point)'. As McKendrick puts it in a delightful version of a poem by Machado:

> To plumb the depths of hell and meet
> ministers, saladins and scholars,
> Marilyn Monroe and Cleopatra,
> the latter naked as the day they died...
> To be steered about by someone who just
> happens to be Virgil, and you like his poems.
> To write as a chisel writes on rock
> so every phrase you write resounds forever:
> ABANDON ALL HOPE ... You first.
> No really I insist please after you.

Beneath the playfulness lies a young poet with a mature sense of purpose. The Machado translation is one of several he deploys skilfully throughout the book to extend his themes. The image of being 'stuck in this nothing ... up to our necks' comes in an adaptation from Montale. This suggests an intelligent reading of the European tradition and an appreciation of what is involved in writing poetry in an age when all the supporting structures of belief are in question. In 'Black Sounds' he creates a compelling picture of the ancient sources as poisoned, primitive and almost impossible to reach: but in 'Frankenstein's Pre-Natal Recollections' he turns the difficulty back upon himself and, by extension, upon anyone living post-Darwin, for whom 'the place of origin was emptiness', who knows only 'the gloomy angel / hunched over slide-rules and a rheostat' and for whom

>   each movement
> is an impossible bridging of fault-lines,
> each thought unprecedented as a tripod
> which must learn to dance upon a tightrope.

New Gen Diary

*The events around January 12th, when the New Generation Promotion was announced, took many people by surprise – not least the New Generation Poets themselves. **Don Paterson**, winner of the 1993 Arvon Poetry Competition, tells of days in* Vogue

When I was ten years old I was obsessed with origami. I wrote a letter to the *Dundee Evening Telegraph* wondering if there was anyone out there with whom I could exchange double crimps and discuss the aesthetic ramifications of the Fred Rohm simplex base. A photographer appeared at the house, and in due course my letter was printed beside an awful photograph of me looking like a girl, below the deathless headline 'Donald is Seeking Fellow Paper-Folders'. Then for twenty years, nothing. Like most of the poets on the New Generation list, I'm a relative media virgin; yes, over the years there have been sticky fumblings with local press and radio, and the custard-stacking hell of a first-night flop that was an appearance on *Kaleidoscope* about a year ago. None of that, however, prepared me for the last couple of weeks. What follows may be read as a gloss on the larger question of whether poetry or poets will ever be ripe for public flotation; the problem, one of them, is that as a poet you're obsessed with getting things exactly right (I still have to draft my holiday postcards and cheque-stubs); for that reason, misquotation is almost the worst thing you can imagine happening to you. As for poetry itself – its great strength lies in its sheer intractability, its inability to be simplified, précised, or transformed. Soon it will suffer all these things; perhaps we should steel ourselves for the results.

Monday, Jan 10th, 7.30am. Doorbell. Postman has more or less destroyed copy of Polygon's *Dream State* book (an anthology of the younger Scottish poets – see page 22) by trying to cram it through the letterbox. I always feel very well disposed towards anthologies I'm in; even so, Donny O'Rourke looks to have done a brilliant job. One or two odd omissions (no M. Imlah, no R. Robertson), but no matter; very good intro, ie it says nice things about me. Then the first letdown of the week. 'Paterson, who also works as a rock musician ...' I am not a rock musician. I am a jazz musician. Not whoopee-cushion jazz where fat men play clarinets out of the sides of their faces. Not wholemeal jazz where coked-up Berkeley graduates play 45-minute polytonal abstractions on the changes of 'I'm Gonna Wash That Man Right Out of My Hair'. It would take too long

to explain. But I am a jazz musician. My one flirtation with 'rock' was a failed audition for 'The Abortions', a Dundee punk band led by a guy who had changed his name by deed poll to Bread Poultice, a Dundee folk-cure for everything from splinters to unwanted pregnancies. 'Uh, wih like yer playin but thi image isny quite right furruz', said Bread, his green unicorn spike wilting a little in apology. I was wearing a school blazer and National Health glasses at the time. God was nudging me in a different direction.

Tuesday, Jan 11th, 9.06am. Board Dundee-King's Cross train, which has been my most reliable postal address for the last few months. Pass the journey writing letters, liana-swinging to the buffet and back, and french-polishing four lines of what, by Peterborough, turns out to be absolutely nothing at all. At Edinburgh Waverley I was feeling like Paul Eluard. Now I feel like Paul Gascoigne. Such is the transformational power of *la poésie*.

2.57pm. Arrive King's Cross. Attempt to phone someone called Isabella Blow ('How do you spell that?' 'B.L.O.W.' 'Oh.') who's organizing a photoshoot for *Vogue*. I kid you not.

4.00pm. Arrive at Mike Donaghy's. We're recording something for the BBC News this evening. Discuss *Poetry Review* questionnaire, like, is it for real? As always on these occasions, suspicion falls on Matthew Sweeney.

7.00pm. Turn up at Hannigan's, a posy Irish pub with pictures of Joyce and Beckett on the walls; they even have a restaurant, bravely trying to do something *haute* with what is generally agreed to be the worst national cuisine in the known universe. The BBC crew turn up with Bill Swainson, The World's Most Reassuring Presence. Bill has the habit of materializing like Obi-Wan Kenobi when you need him most, offering advice, drink, directions, more drink. We talk rubbish, they film it, we play a couple of tunes, they film it. We giggle like two eight-year olds. They film it. How they will make this look good is anybody's guess.

Wed, Jan 12, 8.30am. At last ! Nicholas Wichell, the thinking man's detumescent, says, 'and in a few minutes, poetry goes pop'. Oh fuck *no*. Nicholas is talking over a mute clip of Mike reading to camera while I stroke my chin, trying to look suitably moved.

8.40am. Here goes. First there's a bit from a Radio 1 studio, an actress reading some of Duffy's 'Valentine' over a synth drone. It sounds *horrible*. Then a clip of Simon Armitage, tastefully backlit, leaning over a parapet, the famous fringe lifting and sinking like a crow's wing. He turns to the camera and says something sensible. Bastard. Then, uh-oh, it's us. We're playing a slip-jig from O'Neill's *Irish Traditional Music: A Fascinating Hobby*, reharmonized in the style of late Busoni. It's supposed to look like we're playing a gig here, but if we tried to palm this off on the punters we'd be hitting the pavement before the first round was in. We don't look good. Pasty. The harsh lighting shows up the pink on the collar of my green shirt. My hair is receding alarmingly, something I hadn't really noticed before. Mike says something witty, intelligent, and more or less completely disingenuous. Then there's me reading a bit of a poem, the first bit. This makes about as much sense as broadcasting an excerpt from a joke, but the media are unlikely ever to understand this; as far as they're concerned the most important thing about poetry is its *ambience*, that's to say its ability to confer briefly on the reader a state that feels somewhere between sensitivity and intelligence. *I heard a poem today*, a secret part of them will say to themselves; they will hoard this feeling all day like a shiny sixpence, touching it now and again for luck and reassurance.

In a dubious 'coup' the Beeb have discovered some hopeless, amiable old duffer at the bar who's just had his Collected Poems published. He gets to read one of them. There's no time for anything from Simon or Mike, but auld Jock McSock gets his shot at the bigtime.

11.30am. Show up at Poetry Soc for New Generation press briefing. The place is mobbed. The list of books in the New Gen promotion is stuck up on the wall like the papal blacklist. Mass confusion for the next hour. What the hell am I drinking? Melvyn Bragg shows up: despite having spent the night in a ditch, he rouses himself to deliver a speech that is a small miracle of flattery, diplomacy, and common sense. I've no idea if he meant any of it. I don't care. I bought it all. What a pro. Oddly handsome in the flesh, in a sort of knackered, leonine way. Spend the next half hour talking into microphones, notebooks, tape recorders, and trying to be noticed by *The Late Show*, unsuccessfully. Some bossy dickhead of a photographer for the *Times* suggests that we should all cram into the Poetry Society window for a sort of monkey-enclosure shot. On Sarah Maguire's excellent suggestion, we count to three and give him the collective finger, just as his flash goes off. To my knowledge the shots were not used.

Talk to someone from Radio 1. Her 'naively' straightforward questions catch me offguard and actually provoke a genuine response; for the first time in what seems like an age I find myself in complete agreement with me. 'It's about love and fear and wonder, it's about making the world seem weird as shit again'. Okay, it's naff, but I meant it.

12.30pm. Pub, thank God. Talk to John Osborne and Margaret Busby about notable exclusions from the list. My own feeling, for the record, is that if the list could have been extended by five or six and certain of the criteria relaxed a little, they could all have been accommodated. 'Twenty Seven Youngish More or Less British Poets' doesn't sound so good, I guess. It seems a great shame that poets genuinely deserving wider exposure – Didsbury and Shapcott spring immediately to mind – can't be the beneficiaries of this sort of promotion; perhaps they should have started with them and constructed the criteria retrospectively. If they'd done that, I suppose I wouldn't be on it, so maybe I should just be graceful and grateful and shut up.

Have fight with fellow Dundonian W. N. ('Bill') Herbert about prosody, something to do with the viability of syllabics in English. Burnside and Maguire mediate. Herbert's brain is wired up all wrong so it works three times the speed of anyone else's; this means he usually appears to win every argument, whether he has or hasn't. But this is my subject. Nobody fucks with me on this one. He's losing, and knows it. Bill is sobbing now, and spitefully remarks that this is the only subject I'm capable of getting animated about. I realise, to my utter dismay, he's right. Seriously, though, I'm really proud of us; a random sample of half-a-dozen male and female poets, discussing the nuts and bolts of our trade with an authority and depth of understanding you'd be hard pressed to match in any Eng. Dept. in the country. We'd finally reappropriated what was rightfully ours.

6.30pm. Er ... still here. In the pub. Kathleen Jamie reappears, having shopped, showered, gone home to Newburgh to pick up the mail and come back again. We discuss tomorrow's *Vogue* shoot. We laugh at the rumours of ski-pants and polo-necks.

> *Jamie McKendrick may well be Scottish for Jimi Hendrix, but Jamie has little of his namesake's fashion consciousness*

Maxwell, who will write the article, is smiling strangely.

Thursday, 9.35am. I buy the *Guardian* and the *Independent.* On the front page of the *Guardian* it says: 'The Working Class takes over, p15'. What *fuckwit* said that, I chortled, flicking to the right page. Ha ha ha ha ha ha ha. ha ha ha ha. Ha. Amongst the other gems attributed to yours truly: 'yeah, it's great, none of this stuff is in received standard English (sic) and we don't use any rhetorical language'. Coming from me, that's rich. 'Yeah, none of us have any O levels and we all read American poetry and we're all Scottish and it's like a conversation down the pub.' I'm paraphrasing only slightly. I can't believe I said this shit. I take issue with me point for point: 1) I can count 5 PhDs on the list without trying; 2) Robert Service is a better poet than Frank O'Hara and I keep four remaindered copies of *April Galleons* in my toilet for emergencies; 3) well, okay, half of us *are* Scottish, but that only reflects the higher national IQ; and 4) is too fatuous to dignify with an answer. Send three-and-fourpence, we're going to a dance.

11.00am. Turn up at the Cheese Studios for the *Vogue* thing, along with Simon, Kathleen, Lavinia Greenlaw, Jo Shapcott, and Jamie McKendrick. Why us in particular? We sit around and fidget like six dinner guests in an Agatha Christie, waiting for the host to turn up. It's obvious that this is going to be the *works*; at the end of the vast penthouse studio there's a giant black goalpost heavy with theatrical lighting; behind that, there's one of these enormous, unbroken scrolls of white paper stretching from floor to ceiling. Then, we're introduced to the, er, incomparable Isabella Blow, and Stuart, the photographer, who throughout the afternoon regales me in stage Scotch: 'Hoots mon, kid ye move yer leg a wee muckle, och aye' etc. It's weird, after all these years I still find this totally hilarious.

The place is crawling with about ten flunkeys and hangers-on, all charged with the most minuscule of tasks: film loader, lens wiper, biscuit wallah. Enter Tabitha, an impossible creature in enormous dungarees with a wee caste mark Pritt-stuck to her forehead and only half the requisite number of facial muscles. She exudes what she probably thinks of as a fashionable boredom with the single-minded dedication of a corpse. Tabitha is studying English at the moment, which probably accounts for her present difficulties with it.

> *Would Eliot have done this? Nah. Auden yes. MacDiarmid definitely, and Pound would have turned up an hour early with his own ski-pants*

11.30am. We've just been told we've all got to wear black ski-pants and polo-necks with little two-tone tap-dancer's brogues. There's a shocked silence. Glyn Maxwell is dogmeat. We're left a while to allow the full horror of this sink in.

11.45am. We're lined up like a bunch of twelve year olds waiting for the TB jab. It's me first. I go behind a big screen and put the stuff on, then creep towards the big mirror. I look like across between Max Wall and a bin-liner full of jellyfish. Jamie's next. Jamie McKendrick might well be Scottish for Jimi Hendrix, but Jamie has little of his namesake's fashion consciousness. If it gets cold, Jamie isn't the sort of person who'll put a T-shirt under his shirt. Jamie will just wear two shirts. Nevertheless, he emerges looking like the Olympic solo luge champion, an effect largely due to being 7'4 and wearing a pair of ski-pants originally a foot long. He looks incredible. Simon's less happy. He swears he hears Tabitha say 'if the shit hits the fan, we'll just have to go with the Paul Smith trousers'. This causes me much merriment because we know we'll have to wait 350 years to hear the sentence again. A gorgeous man in designer stubble, pigtails and a frock turns up to do the makeup. The girls spend the next hour behind the screen.

12.30pm. Then the girls, no, women, reappear; they all look intimidatingly stunning. Jo looks like the Statue of Liberty turning up for a step class.

12.45pm. Pose no. 1 is balancing on a stick with a block glued to the end of it, then crossing your legs, the idea being to conceal the stick so it looks like you're sitting in the air. There's something oddly touching in the way we're bracing each other with our fingertips just to stay upright; if one topples, we all will. We keep this up for half an hour, and I still have the imprint of a small rectangle in my arse to prove it. We speculate. Supposing Les Murray had been British and under 40? Imagine Les in a pair of ski-pants, trying to balance on a foot and a half of dowelling. Even the Paul Smith trousers, I suspect, would have been of little comfort to him.

1.15pm. Stuart lets us see the polaroids. Due to the effects of foreshortening, we look like a plate from a medical textbook illustrating a range of spinal deformities. Lavinia and Simon look like midgets. Jamie, being the height he is is relatively unaffected. I look like something from Clive Barker's *Nightbreed*, my head emerging directly from my navel. We break for lunch. Further speculation. Would

Eliot have done this? Nah. Auden yes. MacDiarmid definitely, and Pound would have turned up an hour early with his own ski-pants.

1.30pm. Stuart's flunkeys have constructed something which he thinks is 'kinda Bauhaus' but from here just looks like offcuts from an old Play-Away set. The idea seems to be that we drape ourselves groovily over the white boxes, album-cover stuff. I choose the wrong moment to go to the toilet (an act hindered considerably by my ski-pants): when I get back all the best seats have gone, and the only place left is standing on the top of a six foot box. Stuart comes over with six little black flags. He wants us to hold them, semaphore-style. Simon already near to exasperation, makes a stand. 'Sorry, Sorry, I'm not holding that.' I'm astonished. This is a revelation: I didn't know you were allowed to say no. I've been so conditioned to be grateful for every morsel of publicity that if Stuart had asked me to stick the flag up my arse and wave I would have accepted without demur. While Stuart snaps away I face up to the awful horror of this: by tonight the *Guardian* and *Indie* will be holding the discarded, vinegar-sodden remains of someone's white pudding supper. The half-life of a *Vogue* spread, on the other hand, is something else again. This will live on in dentists' waiting rooms, attics, Blue Peter time-capsules for years to come. I imagine someone coming across the photo in, say, Lavinia's biography in seventy years time (caption: *Vogue*, May 1994. L-R: Jo Shapcott, Kathleen Jamie, L.G., unknown dickhead on box with flag, Simon Armitage, Jamie McKendrick). I feel destined for total obscurity, like the crap one from the Fauves or Les Six that nobody can ever remember. This is strangely comforting. Given my scourge-of-the-middle-classes, hammer-of-the-Oxbridge-hegemony turn yesterday, the irony of finding myself standing in a box dressed like fat chorus-girl is not lost on me. Can I go home now? I want my mother. For the first time in my life I am inordinately conscious of my bottom.

Stuart has produced a bucket of water. 'I think I feel another fuck off coming on', mutters Simon, darkly. 'OK guys, we've let the flags go, but go with me on this one'. He wants me to throw a bucket of water over Simon. I'm quite keen on this, but Simon refuses to play ball. 'Righto', says Stuart, 'just tip the bucket directly in front of you'. 'But Lavinia'll get soaked.' 'No she won't, och aye the noo, trust me on

this one babe'. 1.2.3. I tip the bucket. Stuart clicks away. Lavinia gets soaked. 'That's the one! Ha ha, see yoo Jimmy.' My shame is boundless. I have betrayed the memory of my ancestors. Where's the bread knife.

5.00pm. King's Cross. Pick up the *Glasgow Herald*. Yesterday the photographer dragged us half a mile through Covent Garden in the freezing cold to pose in a stairwell and take 200 exposures of the Scottish contingent. Nice photo. It's a shame my eyes were closed.

Enough. Enough. There has to be a limit to this stuff. Poetry isn't for everybody. Not everyone deserves it. Me and Donaghy are never going to fill Wembley Arena, Mike zipping up the ramp on his motorized skateboard to recite 'Shibboleth' with one foot on the monitor, holding the mike out for the last line as 10,000 adolescents scream 'Maxine! Laverne! Patty!' ('Can't hear yah!' 'Patty!') Poetry isn't the new rock 'n roll, nor was it the old rock 'n roll. Poetry is poetry is poetry. The road to poetry has long been a mess of traffic cones and detours, with no visible sign of any roadworks; it's a matter for celebration that these obstructions have finally gone. The books are in the shops. The shops are in the High Street. We can appeal – if that's the word – directly to the reading public, rather than relying on academics to plead our case whilst simultaneously marginalizing and misinterpreting us through the need to protect the myth of their own expertise. But just because it's dual-carriageway all the way doesn't mean that the destination's any different; poetry is still a place to get lost, mugged, scared, drunk, high, laid and smart in, a strange little town for which no reliable streetplan exists, full of all-night cafés, tiny specialist libraries, tango bars, Zen gardens and Balti houses. Let's keep it that way, huh? But now that we've been led to believe that tangible rewards – in the usual forms of money, sex, and fame – might exist for our efforts, it's inevitable that a few of our number will be tempted to simplify what they do in the hope of maximizing those rewards; or, to extend an already over-extended analogy, pull down the backstreets and put up a mall and a multi-screen in their place. I know this sounds like paranoia, and that no-one is going to raze Venice to build Welwyn Garden City (sorry Glyn), but we must be vigilant. *God, let not our heads be turned.*

> *Poetry is still a place to get lost, mugged, scared, drunk, high, laid and smart in, a strange little town for which no reliable streetplan exists, full of all-night cafés, tiny specialist libraries, tango bars, Zen gardens and Balti houses*

MICHAEL DONAGHY
Errata

MICHAEL DONAGHY WAS BORN TO IRISH PARENTS IN NEW YORK'S BRONX IN 1954, AND EDUCATED at Fordham University and the University of Chicago. He was Poetry Editor of the *Chicago Review* for several years before moving to England in 1985. He works as a musician in an Irish traditional band and also plays with fellow New Gen Don Paterson. His first collection, *Slivers*, was published by Thompson Hill in America in 1985, many of the poems also appearing in his first UK collection, *Shibboleth* (OUP, 1988). The title poem of this book won second prize in the 1987 National Poetry Competition. He won the Whitbread Poetry Prize in 1989. *Errata* was published by OUP in 1993 and reviewed by Michael Hulse in *Poetry Review*, Summer 1993.

Donaghy's music is an integral part of his poetry. Many poems deal with Irish traditional music as refracted through America, but the blues and R&B of Chicago also streak his language with their soulful argot. The fine poem 'Down', for example, crosses the formality learned from Derek Mahon with Chicago South Side: 'Helicopters insect round/Above the burned out cars./Here where the Gospel testified/Between the wars/His harp of darkness cried and prayed/To bottleneck guitars.//Tell me why you's cryin' baby?/I sure would like to know'.

In many respects Donaghy is still an American poet, mining the territory mapped out by poets such as Anthony Hecht, Richard Wilbur and Richard Howard. The search for formal grace in a world that is often savage and graceless is an abiding feature of this tradition, and 'Machines' – the first poem in *Shibboleth* – announces his intention perfectly: 'Dearest, note how these two are alike:/The harpsichord pavane by Purcell/And the racer's twelve-speed bike'. The poem refers to the harmony of the spheres and Dante's heaven and articulates his quest for platonic perfection. Some critics have noted Donaghy's restless trying on of styles between the poles of streetlore and ornate, mannered narrative and his occasional lurches into coyness (his fondness for the word 'Dearest', for example), but Donaghy is an important figure, bridging two worlds of poetry which have much in common and much to learn from each other, but which in recent years, have often refused to communicate. **(PF)**

Michael Donaghy writes:
I want to say that my poems speak for themselves. I expect we all do. They have their own lives to lead. For those of you who don't know my poems, there's a lot of memory in them. Memory and history and music and sex and drinking. I hope you find them memorable – or at least memorizable.

Recently, a hostile reviewer dismissed them like this:

'His poems are not confessional, but it helps to think of a Confessional – a little box with a screen separating two parties.' Think of that screen as the page. A voice seems to come from behind the screen, but if you read the

poems aloud the only voice you hear is your own' (Florence Olsen, *Haymarket*). I can live with that.

Three influential 20th C. Books:
My principal influences aren't 20th century. But since you ask, there's no escaping that lunatic Yeats (*The Tower*). Paul Muldoon redirected me to Frost, his ear, his palimpsest ironies (*Complete Poems*, 1949). For my third choice I considered prose (Borges) or the collected Bishop or MacNeice, but Derek Mahon's *The Snow Party* brought me back to poetry when I thought I'd almost given up.

THREE POEMS BY MICHAEL DONAGHY

Caliban's Books

Hair oil, boiled sweets, chalk dust, squid's ink . . .
Bear with me. I'm trying to conjure my father,
age fourteen, as Caliban – picked by Mr Quinn
for the role he was born to play because
'I was the handsomest boy at school'
he'll say, straight-faced, at fifty.
This isn't easy. I've only half the spell,
and I won't be born for twenty years.
I'm trying for rainlight on Belfast Lough
and listening for a small blunt accent barking
over the hiss of a stove getting louder like surf.
But how can I read when the schoolroom's gone
black as the hold of a ship? Start again.

Hair oil, boiled sweets . . .
But his paperbacks are crumbling in my hands,
seachanged bouquets, each brown page
scribbled on, underlined, memorized,
forgotten like used pornography:
The Pocket Treasury Of English Verse
How To Win Friends And Influence People
30 Days To A More Powerful Vocabulary

Fish stink, pitch stink, seaspray, cedarwood . . .
I seem to have brought us to the port of Naples
midnight, to a shadow below deck
dreaming of a distant island.
So many years, so many ports ago!
The moment comes. It slips from the hold
and knucklewalks across the dark piazza
sobbing *maestro! maestro!* But the duke's long dead
and all his magic books are drowned.

The Tragedies

Upstage, spotlit, the prince soliloquizes
while courtiers ham their business in the dark.
We see you taking snuff, dim improvisers.
We won't remember, but you've left your mark
within the compass of our sense of sight.

It's how we speed down narrow streets and park.
It's how owls reconnoitre fields by night.

And dimmer, in the wings, the age grows vague
and greyly out-of-focus. Children die,
a page reports, in papal war and plague.
We glimpse them out the corner of our eye
and see them without looking, without pain.
We aim our minds like arrows at the Dane.

He dies. *Go bid the soldiers shoot.* Applause
like big wings flapping from an autumn field.
Now, as we glance about, the dark withdraws.
The stage dissolves. The orchestra's revealed
as though the light were rising on a tide
past stalls and circle to the streets outside,
as though the vision centred everywhere.

No animal eye can long survive that glare.
  *And let me speak to the yet unknowing world
  How these things came about.*

                    You caught its eye.
Its talons stretched. A silent wing unfurled.
A shadow glided gently from the sky.

Our Life Stories

What did they call that ball in Citizen Kane?
That crystal blizzardball forecasting his past?
Surely I know the name. Your mum's souvenir
Of Blackpool underwater in winter –
Say we dropped it. What would we say we broke?
And see what it says when you turn it over . . .

I dreamt the little Christmas dome I owned
Slipped my soapy fingers and exploded.
Baby Jesus and the Virgin Mother
Twitching on the lino like dying guppies.
Let's shake this up and change the weather.

Catch! This marvellous drop, like its own tear,
has leaked for years. The tiny ferris wheel has surfaced
in an oval bubble where it never snows
and little by little all is forgotten. Shhh!
Let's hold the sad toy storms in which we're held,
Let's hold them gingerly above the bed,
Bubbles gulping contentedly, as we rock them to sleep,
Flurries aswim by our gentle skill,
Their names on the tips of our tongues.

Rabbitings On

John Updike and Michael Donaghy are both Americans, both writers of grace and wit, but Donaghy finds the writer of the Rabbit saga and Couples sometimes guilty of porno-kitsch and cod concretism:

John Updike,
Collected Poems,
Hamish Hamilton, hbk, £20
ISBN 0 241 00167 6

At his best, John Updike spins a humane, exuberant musical rhetoric from a metaphysical junkheap of bicycle chains, telephone poles, the erection and the Resurrection. His *Collected Poems* is replete with stunningly wrought lines and startling metaphors. 'The Angels', for example, are the great artists and composers who continually remind us that there is a realm 'above this plane of silent compromise'. Above and below, they surround us '... echoing in subway tunnels,/ springing like winter flowers from postcards/ Scotch-taped to white kitchen walls ... burning in memory like leaky furnace doors'. Here he balances passion and wit so adroitly that he earns the rhetorical grandeur of the ending: 'Love us, dead Thrones:/sing us to sleep, awaken our eyes,/ comfort with terror our mortal afternoons'.

But when Updike nods, he snores. His badness, like his sexism, requires a separate study. It's troubling to encounter a writer of Updike's intelligence unable, or unwilling, to distinguish between his best work and his mistakes. More troubling still are the poems that almost made it before the skill took over. For when it comes to the alchemical payoff, when it comes, in short, to the poetry, John Updike rarely bothers.

For the most part, he's cheerfully and graciously aware of this; almost a third of the volume is devoted to light verse, a genre which died off in America, he once remarked, at about the same time dancers in movies stopped going up and down stairs in white tie and tails. In his own light verse he 'strings some similar (sic) things, French inventors, semi-extinct animals, new developments in particle physics, in a kind of necklace of stanzas and steps back pleased'.

> **When Updike nods, he snores. His badness, like his sexism, requires a separate study**

This *bijouterie* is a hallmark of his style, which begs an awkward question: How does he know when he's writing light verse? Unfortunately, he has a formula. A real poem, he tells us in the book's Preface, 'derives from the real (the given, the substantial) world and light verse from the man-made world of information – books, newspapers, words, signs ... a number of entries wavered back and forth across the border'. Most of the book, in fact. Often, the effect is a waste of talent and energy: Fred Astaire attempting to dance *The Rite of Spring*.

Many of the poems feel like alarmingly successful workshop exercises, each hurtling toward its closure like a door slamming: Updike contemplating a windowframe, a stalk of celery, a blowjob. He demonstrates the ease of a Major League pitcher as he lobs us his processed subjects. Here, try this golfball. This wristwatch. I ducked at 'The Beautiful Bowel Movement' ('O spiral Perfection, not seashell nor/ stardust, how can I keep you? With this poem') Was there ever a more brazen case of Cheating the Hangman?

For some poets the enterprise of writing poetry begins with momentarily forgetting that it's impossible. But for a Method Poet like Updike, it's simply a matter of sticking to the formula. Consider the Augustan poets who had only to flesh out ideas in poetic diction and dress them up as nymphs and shepherds. Grainger's or Cowley's elaborate scientific allegories in rhyme are perfectly logical, perfectly ridiculous, perfectly tasteless.

Updike, of course, knows he's being tasteless. He aspires to it. Cowley is to Updike what Shakespeare was to Keats. He even shares with the great James Grainger a poem on rats. 'The villains pass/ with scrabbly traffic noise...' (Updike), 'the whiskered vermin race' (Grainger). And 'Seven Odes To Natural Processes' ploughs remorselessly through Entropy, Crystallization, Evaporation etc for fourteen pages.

'Midpoint' also invokes Augustan mannerism among its many styles (which include photographs from a family album and a cod concretism). It's an ambitious sprawl of a poem but Updike sabotages it with his patented porno-kitsch. In a section where he 'addresses those he has loved' individual women blur into Woman:

you whose breast I soaped
  and you my cock, and your cunt
indivisible from the lather and huge as a purse
                        and the mirror
  giving us back ourselves ...

... and in the Caribbean the night you knelt
to be taken from behind and we were
                    entangled
  with the mosquito netting
and in the woods you let me hold your breasts
  your lipstick all flecked
the twigs dissolved in the sky above and I
                        jerked off
  driving home alone one-handed
singing of you

Object that Updike is not writing – or driving – with due care and attention and he defiantly stares you down, flashing his ironic license. Taste?

I have, alas, no taste –
  taste, that Talleyrand, that ally of the Minimal,
  that foreign-accented intuiter

He concludes 'Taste' by rolling up his sleeves and slapping Nature on the back: 'I want to be like Nature, tasteless, abundant, reckless, cheerful'. Which is cheating, of course. Updike displays more than enough intuition (i.e. taste) to craft a real poem. But that, he seems to say, would be downright UnAmerican. Believe me, if he weren't so busy being reckless, abundant, and cheerful, he might have produced a smaller but weightier collection. His light verse, I should add, is often quite funny.

A BLUFFER'S GUIDE TO POETRY WORKSHOPS

Many of the New Generation poets cut their teeth on poetry workshops. Ian McMillan shows you how to make an instant impact.

Always carry your poems in a big blue folder marked Selected Poems, which should bear your name and address in letraset. Don't worry: nobody will ever ask you who selected them. As well as your folder of poems, you will need a spiral bound notebook marked *Notes for Future Poems*. This should be a plain notebook, and on no account should be called *Inspiration*. Other essential equipment includes pens, pencils, and a marker pen, which should be laid out on the table next to your folder and notebook when you sit down.

If the poetry workshop you're attending has requested photocopied poems for circulation to the rest of the group, on no account bring any. This means that the group will have to listen to you delivering your poem, thus giving you chance to preface it with explanatory notes.

When it's the time to comment on someone else's poem, wait until somebody is speaking, then interrupt them with the kind of phrase that makes them think you just can't hold yourself in any longer. Phrases like 'This poem made me shiver: it was as though a ghost had passed over my grave' or 'God, I'm glad we're poets not photographers' will do. At this point it's often good to wipe imaginary sweat from your brow or (if you're a man) shift uncomfortably in your chair to show that the poem is so powerful it has given you an erection.

Cultivate noises. The obvious ones are MMMMMM at the end of someone's poem, (make sure it is the end by glancing at the text beforehand) and HAH! halfway through a stanza, to show that you are understanding some esoteric point the writer has made. Less obvious, but just as effective, are nonsense words in the silence that follows a poem: 'Giddy' or 'Norfolk' are favourites of mine.

Finally, always leave before the end of the workshop. Drop a name as you go, eg: 'Simon's ringing me at ten', or 'You can't keep Carol Ann waiting'.

As you leave, appear to be struck by something in the room (a beam of light, the shape of a chair, the hair of the man in the Donald Duck tie) and scribble a few words in your notebook; at the door, turn and say 'Well, you never know when she'll strike, do you?'

Happy workshopping!

SARAH MAGUIRE
Spilt Milk

SARAH MAGUIRE WAS BORN IN LONDON IN 1957. SHE TRAINED AS GARDENER BEFORE READING ENGLISH at the University of East Anglia. She has lived in Notting Hill for 20 years and has taught creative writing in a men's prison and at the London Lighthouse, a hospice for HIV-sufferers. Her work first appeared in *New Chatto Poets 2*. *Spilt Milk,* her first collection, was published by Secker & Warburg in 1991, and reviewed by Ian McMillan in *Poetry Review*, Spring 1992.

'I have entered that domestic season', begins 'A Cherry Tree', and metaphorical and sometimes literal seasons and climates, both domestic and global, pervade Sarah Maguire's work. She writes of the brooding of sultry cities, of the Chernobyl radiation cloud, of trunks being emptied, exuding their 'Stiff aroma of new cloth'. She is a travelled poet and what she sees is riddled with signs and symbols: even when at home she discerns portents in the physical environment. In a house damaged by frost the sense of fragility is transferred to the 'meniscus on the cold tap' forming and bursting. A failed love affair is projected onto a shared meal, *mushrooms à la grecque,* which didn't go down well and had to be expelled.

Her imagery tends towards a crossover of the senses: during the Notting Hill carnival 'oil drums are beaten to chromatics', catching both the sound of the drums and the glints that shine off them. Bernard O'Donoghue has noted how often contamination and pollution appear in her poems and one could widen this to include blurring in general, one thing melting into another – matter penetrated by desire. She is more interested in cultural theory than most of the New Generation (see page 69) but this does not intrude in any obvious way on her work, which stays close to the traditional 20th-century blues of rooms, townscapes and relationships. **(PF)**

Sarah Maguire writes:
Poems are like dreams: in them you put what you don't know you know.

(Adrienne Rich)

Some of my poems might well start from autobiographical events, but the formal demands of poetry mean they can't ever be 'confessional'. The 'accuracy with respect to the structure of reality' in poetry (Wallace Stevens) is the accuracy of prosody. There's no 'me' you can know from my poetry.

Is anything (*pace* Elizabeth Bishop) harder to master than the art of losing? In *Black Sun: Depression and Melancholia* Julia Kristeva writes that 'artistic *style* imposes itself as a means of countervailing the loss of other and of meaning', because 'the [poetic] construction becomes a substitute for the lost ideal in the same way

as it transforms the woeful darkness into a lyrical song'. I want to transgress the boundaries of the lyric tradition, with its connotations of hermetic intimacy, without employing the exhortations of polemic, without losing sensuality or richness of language. 'There is no history outside its subjective realisation ... just as there is no subjectivity uncoloured by the history to which it belongs' (Jacqueline Rose). For women to write poetry, to authorise desire, it's necessary to move from being the object of poetry to being its subject.

Three Influential 20th C. Books:
Adrienne Rich, *The Fact of a Doorframe: Poems Selected & New 1950-84*; Elizabeth Bishop, *Complete Poems*, Sylvia Plath, *Collected Poems*.

Postmodernism

Sarah Maguire on the byword for late-twentieth century culture ...

Q: Does the term 'postmodernism' have any useful meaning for you?

A: Yes, as a critical-theoretical term referring to a specific historical moment: i.e. late capitalism characterized by flexible accumulation and dizzying speed-time compression.

What worries me is the way that the complexities of postmodernism have been reduced to a matter of *style,* specifically a kind of excess of reference and signification, which undermines any more radical, critical analysis which would situate postmodernism within the context of late capitalism. This 'style' is then used to tick off certain poems and poets as being postmodernist or not, which strikes me as being deeply fatuous. If we're going for the slickness of a 'postmodernism = citation without quotation' definition, then my own work is hardly exuberant enough. Stylistically, for example, it could be argued that *The Waste Land* is postmodernist, yet its deeper concerns with the search for a redemptive, all-inclusive myth mark out its modernist concerns. It seems to me to be more useful to interrogate the philosophical assumptions embedded in and motivating aesthetic representations: 'deconstructing' them. On this analysis, much 'feminist' poetry reiterates inscriptions of the 'eternal feminine' as conservative as those put forward by Jean-Jacques Rousseau (from whom, if they did but know, much of their politics is derived).

I'm concerned with a more profound understanding of postmodernism which, following the collapse of various modernist meta-narratives in the wake of World War II, combined with changes in the means of production (the end of Fordism) and access to education of hitherto excluded groups, led to the Civil Rights Movement and the Women's Movement in the 'sixties, which in turn inaugurated a new respect and attention to *otherness*. It's this aspect of postmodernism which I feel most engaged with, and it's one which I think explains the historical moment of the NGP: the 'democratization' of the poetry élite is inseparable from an understanding of post-modernism's relation to 'others'.

In other words, I think there are 'left' and 'right' versions of postmodernism. The former (at its best)

> **Frolicking in the boundless ocean of contingency is not an activity open to the (increasing numbers) of poor, homeless and exploited**

places a postcolonialist and feminist stress on difference and otherness which, whilst emphasizing the deconstruction of meta-narratives (such as notions of gender and race) can retain a materialist and political analysis of inequality and injustice. The 'right' version of postmodernism, whilst having a similar stress on the deconstruction of metaphysics, revels unashamedly in the seamless free-play of signifiers which leads to an idealisation of the signifier deprived of the signified. But frolicking in the boundless ocean of contingency is not an activity open to the (increasing numbers) of poor, homeless and exploited. The unbridled relativism of certain aspects of postmodernism strikes me as being deeply reactionary, the freeplay of signifiers having more in common with so-called 'free' trade and the free-play of money markets than its promulgators would perhaps like us to believe. I worry about the replacement of ethics with aesthetics (which led to the election of Ronald Reagan for example). I worry about the lack of concern with such essential universal metaphysical concepts such as truth and justice. I worry about the (apparent) lack of politics in some postmodernism – which is itself a mask for a reactionary agenda and, in fact, a very political stance.

Two other factors strike me as interesting. One is an increasing interest in *difficulty*. Various art forms have gained popular support recently which hitherto had been seen as élitist and 'difficult' (jazz is a good example), an interest which at first glance might seem to challenge the notion of the postmodern consumer society of 'three-minute culture'. The other is the profound unlinearity of poetry. Helen Vendler writes that poetry 'insists on a spooling, a form of repetition, the reinscribing of a groove, the returning upon an orbit already traced. Lyric poetry – for all its plot, its logic, its conclusions – is profoundly unlinear. It does not advance' (Introduction to the Faber *Contemporary American Poetry*). This seems to me to be linked to the notion of difficulty and to a shift towards metaphor and away from metonymy [an aspect standing for the whole, as in 'The White House' referring to the US Administration]. Consumer culture is, by definition, metonymic otherwise consumption would cease.

THREE POEMS BY SARAH MAGUIRE

The Invisible Mender

(My First Mother)

'For whom do you write? For the dead whom thou didst love' – John Berryman

I'm sewing on new buttons
to this washed silk shirt.
Mother of pearl,
I chose them carefully.
In the haberdashers on Chepstow Place
I turned a boxful over
one by one,
searching for the backs with flaws:
those blemished green or pink or aubergine,
small birth marks on the creamy shell.

These afternoons are short,
the sunlight buried after three or four,
sap in the cold earth.
The trees are bare.
I'm six days late.
My right breast aches so
when I bend to catch a fallen button
that strays across the floor.
Either way,
there'll be blood on my hands.

Thirty seven years ago you sat in poor light
and sewed your time away,
then left.
But I'm no good at this:
an anemone of blood gathers on my thumb, falls
then widens on the shirt like a tiny, opening mouth.

I think of you like this –
as darkness comes,
as the window that I can't see through
is veiled with mist
which turns to condensation
slipping down tall panes of glass,
a mirror to the rain outside –
and I know that I'll not know
if you yet are mending in the failing light,
or if your hands (as small as mine)
lie still now, clasped together, underground.

Heavenly Body

I could stake out the summer at my kitchen window:
   scanning the street,

watching for the scarlet flare of your Mercedes at my kerb.
   Since St Swithin's Day

it's pissed down. On August 12th the world's astronomers
   observed the Perseids,

expectant that Swift-Tuttle's comet dust would storm
   to starlight.

But in Notting Hill the clouds occlude the heavens;
   the passing cars

in darkness turn anaemic, their lights a sallow blur
   along the seething road.

Proof

Your abandoned bottle of Russkaya vodka lies in my icebox,
Cold as a gun; it will chill but not freeze,
The slow distillation latent beneath the iced glass.

The Craftsperson's Contract

by Sarah Maguire

New Virago Poets,
Melanie Silgardo and Janet Beck (eds),
Virago, £5.99, ISBN 1 85381 585 3
Katie Donovan,
The Watermelon Man,
Bloodaxe, £5.95, ISBN 1 85224 215 9
Poetry Introduction 8,
Faber, £6.99, ISBN 0 571 16889 2
Fergus Allen,
The Brown Parrots of Providencia,
Faber £5.99, ISBN 0 571 17011 0

1990 saw the publication of Bloodaxe's exciting anthology of *New Women Poets*, many of whom have since gone on to considerable success (Elizabeth Garrett, Lavinia Greenlaw, Jackie Kay, and Eva Salzman to name but four). Carol Rumens, who edited the collection, attributed the appearance of so many new, skilful women poets to two factors. Firstly, 'the Women's Movement, and the literary revolution to which it led'. And secondly, a new-found confidence in tackling the 'exacting apprenticeship' to the complex and demanding craft of writing poetry.

New Virago Poets
Whilst the influence of the Women's Movement is strongly evident in the *New Virago Poets* anthology, sadly, very few of them display evidence of even the odd day-release course spent grappling with the

'exacting apprenticeship' of their chosen literary genre. And what damages the least successful of these poems so fatally is precisely their authors' failure to appreciate the technical demands of poetry: to grasp that, without an awareness of structure and form, personal experience remains hermetically personal, and political comment comes over as crass polemic.

Throughout, the anthology is marred by language which is flaccid, which is lacking in texture or tension, and which either becomes mired in bathos – 'My coffee no doubt exploits / peasants in Nicaragua. / I drink it anyway' ('Escape to Shanghai', **Jill Dawson**), or is desperately hyper-inflated into trite poeticisms – 'Cupping his surly, power-hungry spume / into my lap / I no longer dream of wedding robes' ('Making Love to Poseidon', **Linda Rose Parkes**).

Not only does language itself remain flat and unchallenged by the bulk of these writers, but they frequently reiterate the worst stereotypes of femininity, offering intellectually sloppy images of the 'eternal feminine'. Poems about maternity and menstruation seem to conjure up clichés with apparent effortlessness: 'The belly of blood is calling / It is roaring for the belly of another pressed against it // roaring to be loved / roaring for its own unborn children // And it roars and it roars' ('In the Tiger Cage', **Christian McEwan**), as do many poems dealing with animals, mythology and nature.

That said, there *are* some good poets in the collection, such as **Moniza Alvi** (whose precise language and delicate ironies are very out of place here), **Pascale Petit**, **Jackie Wills**, and **Jenny Vuglar**. **Briar Wood** is the only poet to appear in both the Bloodaxe and the Virago anthologies; here, I felt that her technical ability was not being stretched quite enough by her subject matter, though her dry wit remained very welcome. Of the poets I'd not read before I was most impressed by **Jane Draycott** who not only thoroughly understood the function of line breaks, but also displayed considerable powers of analysis and insight into her chosen subjects. 'Braving the Dark', a moving sequence of poems about her brother who died of Aids, deals with this difficult issue with restraint and command:

> Passive, your glove allows me to enter
> its five black-soft tunnels:
> the tips however remain uninhabited,
> your fingers having been longer than mine.

Katie Donovan

Sadly, many of the faults bedevilling the least competent of the *New Virago Poets* have infected Katie

Donovan's *The Watermelon Man*. I enjoyed reading this book at the beginning. Donovan writes simply and easily, her relaxed, unpretentious language uses some arresting images – 'the sea is a bath / of salty diamonds' ('Achill') – and she's good at sensual description or the evocation of place. But I wanted her to push harder, to analyse rather than simply record experiences, to move from charming similes into challenging metaphors, to widen her perceptions beyond what is immediately perceived. I often had the feeling that something larger provoked particular poems – which was then left unexplored. 'Husk', in which –

> Emptied of adventure
> we return from long days
> to find a grey husk
> clinging to the cornice –
> a small, perfect bulb
> with a hole at the top.

– seemed a lost opportunity; the husk remains just that, expertly described but nothing more than 'delicate / fibrous remains'.

'Writing the body', an injunction made by the French feminist thinker Helène Cixous, is a task which many women writers have begun to explore, bringing into language huge areas of experience hitherto ignored or silenced. And whilst I agree with the importance of this project, I don't think it's enough simply in itself. Donovan can be commended for the boldness of her writings about the female body (there's a good deal of wetness in this book, a lot of pissing and bleeding) but her poems are rather like the first stages of consciousness-raising groups in the '70s where women experienced the emotional release of talking about their subjective experiences before moving on to begin to contextualize and explore them.

This lack of analysis of sensual meanings leads her to make the unforgivable error of trotting out deeply offensive stereotypes of black male sexuality in 'Black Man'. Here, the man 'is a jungle cat / in city clothes', 'a prowling shadow', whereas the white woman who desires him (civilization incarnate) in her 'beads and spectacles' lives a life which is 'Flaccid and purposeless / ... crying out for depth'. Sentiments which would not be out of place in the *Sun*.

Poetry Introduction 8

All the eight poets in Faber's *Poetry Introduction 8* have definitely reached advanced City & Guilds in the poetic apprenticeship stakes and some show positive signs of achieving 'craftsperson' status very soon. **Nick Drake**'s poems have a quiet elegance. He writes intelligently and thoughtfully of incongruities and displaced persons as an observer at a distance – 'To the Partisan Folk Dance Group of Czechoslovakia' concerns their performance in the Queen Elizabeth Hall and then comes crashing back 'to the hard ground / of common sense' in his witty philosophical excursion on 'Dr Johnson's Bicycle'.

The movement of **Jane Duran**'s poems is unpredictable and original. She uses some wonderfully vivid images, such as a plane 'pulling up' being compared to 'a scarf through a ring' ('The Mere Pleasure of Flying'). In 'The Pumpkin at Halloween' her niece 'dug the pumpkin out, / peeked into its mathematics' which once 'lay in a field / edible and quilted / chiming softly'. She manages to write about the female reproductive system without invoking cliché in 'Termination for Fetal Abnormality'.

Christine Fearnside tackles the painful subject of her mother's Alzheimer's disease with tact and courage:

Her voice moves ahead
witch-like in its croaking,
put on like dressing-up
to be the funny woman.
                    ('The Prisoner')

'A March Day in the Alps' displays a Martian tendency to observe nature through domestic images: 'Above us hanging smooth / somewhere are cleanest sheets, / old slopes turned side to middle'.

Shelah Florey's tone is so restrained as to sometimes slip into a degree of flatness and understatement that fails to do justice to her subject matter, as in her poem about the Gulf War. I felt she was holding herself back at times, a restraint perhaps exacerbated by her clipped, short lines. I'd like her to take her own advice in 'Something Left to Show for It': 'Being roughed up a bit / Intruded upon / Isn't always the disaster / We like to pretend'.

Beatrice Garland's 'Postcard' is an effective subversion of the traditionally anthropomorphic nature poem; here empirical observations are undercut by uncertainty:

I noted them down, not knowing what they
                                    meant
or if anything at all had really happened;
only a state of mind in which eyes, opened
by solitude, could see the lives that other
creatures made.

Her tactile images are particularly impressive: 'I pull my fists back inside the cuffs / and hold my

new generation poets

1993
forward
poetry
prize
whitbread
poetry
award

carol ann
DUFFY

MEAN TIME £6.95

ANVIL

thumbs for comfort. No one sleeps' ('Soldier') and 'a face / wiped dry impatiently, too hard / with someone else's handkerchief' ('Rain'). Her images are effective not merely through sensual evocation but because she uses them to provoke insight.

The very wonderful Ian Duhig must be the first of the New Generation Poets to generate a school, the founding pupil of which is **John Goodby**. Goodby's 'Eighteen Eighteen' is an explicit *hommage* to his master, complete with clumped glottals and abundant scatology; Goodby's version even uses the Duhig meta-trope of the conundrum of Irish identity. Like the original (hardly a postmodern label, I know, but I'm prepared to sacrifice ideological niceties on the altar of truth in this instance). Goodby flaunts an impressively arcane knowledge through a florid use of proper nouns which, decontextualized, are jolted out of their settled meanings into the free-fall of linguistic play. 'In the Tropical House' demonstrates the flight of butterfly signifiers from their traditional signifieds with his typical confidence and humour:

> You might be a Painted Jezebel on the bridge
> above the toy waterfall. I consider it, still
> alighting from or on those harder names:
> Red Pierrot, Sulphur Emigrant, the Great
> Duffer.

'I can't speak your language' writes **Roddy Lumsden** in 'Kippis' and his socially diverse poems are full of miscommunications and the subversion of accepted order, often revealing the menace hidden in social situations. In 'Vanishing' a magician's apprentice 'slams a back-stage door' and walks out on a vanishing trick; in 'The Governor's Dog' a prisoner made paranoid by being held under an oppressive regime tries 'to talk their language' but is offered the test of walking the governor's dog, not as innocent exercise but to see how far he'll go. The controlled irony of these two situations is transmuted into explicit humour in 'Twenty Haiku for my Dentist': 'You ask me to take / a heavy bite. Peep inside / my cheek now, voyeur'.

Maurice Riordan explores the social complexities of domestic interiors with poise and delicacy, frequently investigating the collision between two worlds, the strange disjunctions and gaps in quotidian reality. 'Rural Electrification 1956' is about 'our poleman' who brings stories of other, distant electrifications, 'so that the lights of Piccadilly / were swaying among the lamps of fuchsia, / before he disappeared into the earth'. His opening poem,

the elegant sonnet 'Ghosts', begins: 'I call it home: this house where I'm a guest' and the bulk of these poems are concerned with what exactly constitutes the nature of 'home' : a place seen as vulnerable to fantasies of crisis and abandonment ('Time Out') and to marital discord, making 'the plain altar still fit for household ceremonies' ('The Table') an uncertain object of desire.

Fergus Allen

Fergus Allen's *The Brown Parrots of Providencia* is an exciting and intellectually demanding first collection which is reminiscent of Wallace Stevens, both in its clipped, polysyllabic diction and extraordinarily exotic, arcane language, and also in its philosophical rigour. Allen, like Stevens, is concerned with the metaphysics of perception and the negotiation of shared, social meanings. In 'Aside', 'The liver-coloured dog halts and looks up / Through the one-way mirror of his pale eyes / And writes me off'. The poet wants to be recognized, given meaning: 'Difficult not to scold at all these beings / Who sense that one does not figure in their futures' but he withdraws into his 'helmet of invisibility', warning, 'do not look to me' when 'the looters swarm through the old town / With stones and petrol'.

In these poems, the natural is a contested site of meanings. In 'Other' the poet's cat, 'the familiar that an hour ago / Flatteringly weaved and purred around my ankles' now is 'Weighing me up with his incurious eyes – / The slits of an armoured car would show more interest'. And all is not what it seems in the highly unnatural world of 'Shopping'. The poet, caught in a postmodern nightmare of excess – 'so many / Shades of taste that mesmerize and are gone', recognizes that 'Something goes on out there, beyond the bland / Messages of the pink and sweet and cool'.

Matching the intelligence of these poems is the force of their language and form. The breadth and precision of Allen's vocabulary is staggering (the book should carry a warning that it's not to be read without at least a *Shorter OED* in attendance). There's much play and humour throughout, from the gently ironic 'Necropolis' to the lugubrious tones of a (resting, ageing) 'Actor in Mirror' and the bitterly sardonic insults of 'Foreign Relations':

> Within the sum of words, there are words
> From which we all, well, most of us,
> Start back like a mangabey
> From an exploding seed-pod.
> But your name is my private bugaboo.

JOHN BURNSIDE
The Myth of the Twin

JOHN BURNSIDE WAS BORN IN DUMFERMLINE, FIFE, IN 1955. HIS FIRST VOLUME, *THE HOOP* (CARCANET, 1988) won a Scottish Arts Council Book Award. He has subsequently published *Common Knowledge* (Secker & Warburg, 1991) and *Feast Days* (Secker & Warburg, 1992) and his work has been anthologized in *The New Poetry*, the *Faber Book of 20th Century Scottish Poetry* and *Dream State*. His new collection, *The Myth of the Twin* (Cape), is reviewed by Ian McMillan on page 77.

John Burnside is a poet after George Eliot's heart, obsessed with 'the other side of silence' – a realm in which we can hear the grass grow and a bird's heart beat. This hypersensitivity has proved to be prolific, resulting in four books in six years. His first, *The Hoop*, feeds on Celtic myth and is rich in 'pagan' symbolism but his later work blends in Christian (specifically Catholic) iconography to create a unique spiritual perspective. Burnside's essential subject is the soul's experience of the natural world. His poetry is ambient, evoking atmosphere in immaculately plain language and with gently modulated rhythms. Human beings tend towards insubstantiality – often they are ghostly presences flickering across solid landscapes, wraiths for whom 'Life is a mist/where there is always something else to find'; in contrast, the natural world is worshipped with a lover's tenderness and attention to sensual detail. Burnside's 'nature' is a mythologized space in which 'souls we almost are/almost emerge', and claims on behalf of his intrinsic 'Scottishness' are dubious; he is less concerned with cultural specifics than with shyly approaching The Absolute. His ability to make abstractions vivid is remarkable (eg, an angel's 'muscular wings'). In the title poems of *The Myth of the Twin*, the soul reproduces by splitting in half – a kind of metaphysical mitosis which allows 'otherness' to be graphically represented in the image of the poet's non-identical twin. Burnside's poetic voice, though intensely lyrical, is never that of the egotistical 'I', his work prioritizing inspired commonality over individual insight. **(KJ)**

John Burnside writes:
My work is concerned with a number of recurrent themes – with continuity; with the mysterious quality of the natural world and the moments of revelation that sometimes come to those of us who appear to live on the edge of that world, in the suburbs and in small towns and villages; with notions of identity – as isolate individual with a shifting sense of self, and as member of a community of the living and the dead; with the landscape of the suburbs and the countryside.

I am a Scot by birth, with some Irish blood; I was brought up as a Catholic and I am still fascinated by the imagery of the Pagan/Christian stories of my childhood. I am not very much interested in the public poem (at least, not for the present). I am concerned with the private (as opposed to personal) utterance, with the poem as a way of finding or creating order in the world, or rather, of finding the world itself, in its full richness. I see poetry as a discipline in the old sense of the world, a life's work, a way of finding a place in the world and ultimately as a (sometimes dark) celebration of kinship, death, regeneration and love.

Three influential 20th C. books:

I would not claim influence on my work, but I have enjoyed: Wallace Stevens, *Selected Poems*; W.B. Yeats *Collected Poems*; Geoffrey Hill, *King Log*, and much Spanish poetry (Jimenez, Lorca, Guillen, etc).

THREE POEMS BY JOHN BURNSIDE

A private life

I want to drive home in the dusk
of some late afternoon,

the journey slow, the tractors spilling hay,
the land immense and bright, like memory,

the pit towns smudges of graphite,
their names scratched-out for good: Lumphinnans;

Kelty. I want to see
the darkening rooms, the cups and wireless sets,

the books where I learned how language
happened, how the appleseed decodes

colour and form; I want the lamps and empty playing fields,
the soft men walking home through parks and streets

and quiet women coming to their doors,
then turning away, their struck lives gathered around them.

The new husband

The home I pretend to miss:
ice in the grass and drifts of rotting leaves,
or snowfalls all morning – the air in our room a surprise,
like the presence of birds,

and the sense of another life, that persists
when I go out into the yard
and the cattle stand round me, obstinate and dumb.
At times I have wakened again from someplace
lucid and warm,

a house we have made together, a neatness
of gestures and words, as if we had kept our dreams
to blend their inward streets and holly trees,
and heaven – a figment of love – is somewhere else,
but here is real, where marriages begin.

Convert

I knew what I should choose,
the Lady Days and wet chrysanthemums,
the dressing games we played at Halloween,

but I wanted a mask for love,
the cold at the foot of the stairwell
and needles of ice and milk, like the taste of blood.

I wanted the penance that faded
for days, in the crusted rags
beyond the church, amongst the hazel trees;

the smell of something broken on my skin
at Candlemas; a sprinkling on the hearth
of water or salt, where the dead were surrendered to fire,

and I heard them falling away, in the frosted earth,
a noise like the silence that falls when you finish singing.

Breathing into the Fire

Ian McMillan on the mysterious stillness at the heart of John Burnside's poetry

John Burnside,
The Myth of the Twin,
Cape, £7.00,
ISBN 0 224 03894 X

John Burnside's senses work splendid overtime all the way through this book: 'Our village has been spilled across the fields' ('Cures'), 'but this is my only parish, a space without chairs or bells/ and an altar that smells of mice/ in the wet-weather dark' ('Owlpen'). In the first poem in the collection, 'Halloween', Burnside sets out his creed, his method of alchemy: 'Stooping to a clutch of twigs and straw/ to breathe a little life into the fire'.

The landscapes in the book are often harsh, as in 'The Pit Town in Winter': 'Everything would vanish in the snow,/ fox bones and knuckles of coal/ and dolls left out in the gardens,/ red-mouthed and nude', but the harshness is softened by Burnside's belief that this landscape and the people who inhabit it are (rather like the similar Nottinghamshire landscape and people in some of Peter Sansom's poems) fit and proper subjects for poetry: 'careful, narrow-footed souls,/become the creatures of a sudden light,/amazed at how mysterious they were'. Although a lot of nature finds its way into these poems – 'A litter of chestnuts and eggs;/a linnet's nest; a bread mould in a jar;/ apples like magnets, wrapped in a film of rain' – the real theme is closer to humanity that your average nature poem: 'reveal us all as shivers in the wind/ gusted on woods and wheatfields after rain'.

Given that, some of the shivers in the wind are celebrated in some excellent unsentimental portraits of unspectacular family lives –

There is something in his face
of death accepted:

a recognised form, like the shadow that comes
to the door,
and is only the cat.
('A Photograph of my Grandfather, c. 1961')

– and 'sat together, bound in tea and starch,/un-
bending in the long accomplishment/of permanence,
of choosing to be still' ('My Grandparents in 1963').

The poems are full of places I've been to and can
recognize, and you can't always say that about
poems of place: 'The streets are waiting for a snow/
that never falls' ('Dundee'), and 'The moonlight is
suddenly large: a brightness on the fields that only
shows/ when this house dims' ('Uley, Glos'). Some
themes recur: angels, chrysalises, two poems on the
idea of the twin, and way back like remembered
dreams I can detect the influences of Norman MaCaig
and Ken Smith, the latter in Burnside's tendency to
plunge straight in: 'Say it moved when you moved;
/a softness that rose in the ground when you walked,
or a give in your step' ('The Myth of the Twin').

There was an early review of *Waiting For Godot*
that said 'Nothing Happens, Twice', and in these
poems Burnside's achievement is to make nothing
happen again and again and again. This can be a
little disconcerting on first reading the book,
because I've become used to poems that are full of
action, poets coming on like Mr. Motivator, slim
volumes like exercise videos with acknowledge-
ments. Burnside's stillness contains great truths
about ordinary people:

If I switched off the light
I would see him out in the yard,
tending a fire by the hedge,
raking the windfalls and leaves
from a different year,

a ghost in his smoke-coloured shirt ...
('Variation on a theme of Wallace Stevens')

The stillness doesn't convey self-absorption, but
gives many of the poems (and I'm not being patronizing here, I'm being the opposite) the quality of
much-loved photographs kept in handbags or biscuit tins, or super-8 home movies projected on the
kitchen wall:

a name for the gap between margins,
for siftings and scattered remains,
for rising at night, in the moments I share with
the dead,
and making my place in their house, an echo,
singing.

A GUIDE TO REVIEWERSPEAK

*People tend to get tongue-tied in front of poetry, including the critics. Here is a brief
guide to allow you to decode some of the more common obfuscations.*

'Repays repeated reading' – I didn't understand it first time and I'm never going to
read it again.

'Sparky and streetwise' – uses words like
'schtum', 'prial', 'pelf', 'sashay'.

'Deals with the eternal themes: love, sex,
and death' – a poet of flagrant narcissism
who can't be bothered to bone up on the
outside world.

'Has a telling eye for detail' – is a pedant.

'Risk-taking' – every day he/she courts
death by mixing of metaphors, mauling of
the stanza, and trochee-jumping.

'Eclectic' – has no ideas of his/her own.

'A new more personal note' – the poet is in
love and we're going to have to sit through
a blow by blow account of it.

'Warm, vibrant sensuality' – the poet is my
lover.

'Hysterically emotional/cruelly indifferent
to others' feelings' – the poet *was* my lover.

'Uncompromising' – dares to be rude about
Mrs Thatcher.

'An essential writer' – we have to keep
reminding ourselves that he/she is still alive.

'An antidote to the spiritual void of the
times' – much ado about dolphins, dousing
and menstrual myths.

BIFF

The Louts of Literature
(In Essence, A Just So Story)

Gavin Ewart on Gawain, Guinness, and Rugby Songs ...

Long ago, O Best Beloved, in the High and Far-Off Times, a poem was a long singy thingy. When 'Omer smote 'is bloomin' lyre, it had most to do with tribal bloodshed. But, most completely, it had nothing to do with Rhyme.

The Anglo-Saxons never used rhyme (though the monks in the Middle Ages did make use of it in Latin hymns). Instead they used alliteration:

> In a somer seson,   whan soft was the sonne,
> I shop me in shroudes,   as I a shepe were,
> In habit as an heremite   unholy of workes,
> Went wide in this world   wondres to here.

This is the beginning of Langland's *Vision Of Piers The Plowman*, a 14th Century dream-allegory, where the narrator falls asleep on the Malvern Hills on a May morning – disguised however as a shepherd and not as a sheep, as the uninstructed reader might imagine. In the unreconstructed low life of the time, Glutton staggers about drunk:

> Til Gloton had iglobbed   a galon and a gille.
> His guttes gone gothely   as two gredy
>   sowes;
> He pissed a potel   in a Pater-noster-while,
> And blew his rounde ruwet   at his rigge-bone
>   ende,
> That alle that herde that horn   held her nose
>   after,
> And wisheden it had be wexed   with a wisp of
>   firses.

Here, remembering the lager louts and the other exploits of tabloid alliteration, we might also remember Carol Ann Duffy's *Sun* headline writer: 'I like to think that I'm a sort of poet/ for our times. My shout. Know what I mean?' Indeed, puns and alliteration are the breath of life to the writers of slogans and headlines: 'Labour isn't working', 'Up Yours, Delors!' Even rhyme. Poetry doesn't seem very far distant.

Rhyme didn't appear in any serious Eng. Lit. kind of way until *Sir Gawain and the Green Knight* (see p. 29). Here the rhymed part of each stanza follows the alliterative section. This passage describes how Arthur demands his bardic due (a tall story) at one of his banquets:

> But Arthur would not eat until all were
>   served.
> He was charming and cheerful, child-like and
>   gay,
> And taking life lightly, little he loved
>
> Lying down for long or lolling on a seat,
> So robust his young brain and his beating
>   blood.
> However, something else now had his
>   attention:
> His noble announcement that he never would
>   eat
> On such a fair feast-day till informed in full
> Of some unusual adventure, as yet untold,
> Of some momentous marvel that he might
>   believe,
> About ancestors, or arms, or other high theme;
> Or till a stranger should seek out a strong
>   knight of his,
> To join with him in jousting, in jeopardy to lay
> Life against life, each allowing the other
> The favour of Fortune, the fairer lot.
> Such was the King's custom when he kept
>   court,
> At all famous feasts among his free retinue
>   In hall
> So he throve amid the throng,
> A ruler royal and tall,
> Still standing staunch and strong –
> The year being young withal.

This, of course, unlike the extract from *Piers Plowman*, is a modern version. What Arthur gets is not a verse epic but the supernatural visit of the Green Knight. After Sir Gawain has cut his head off with an axe, the Knight rides off with his head in his hand and Sir Gawain and the King, both happy enough, are given double helpings of everything ('Double portions of each dainty in dignified style,/ All manner of meat') in recognition of a good day's work. Gawain is in no way upset by the thought that in one year's time he has sworn to allow the Green Knight a free swipe at *him*.

This may all be scholarly, élitist, snobbish. Use the pejorative adjectives to hand. But it does show how the poetic tricks of 1340-1400 (the dates of Chaucer and of the Green Knight) haven't yet vanished from popular culture. Even nearer to what might be thought of as 'highbrow' poetry are the products of the advertising agencies; this was especially true when there was only press advertising. With television commercials, the visual image became predominant, yet jingles and slogans have never quite lost their power. Jingles had their heyday in the Fifties (Murraymints, Pepsodent, etc.), though they have now lost ground as against slogans, which are always with us.

When I joined S.H. Benson as a copywriter trainee in 1952, in the days when it was still the foremost British agency, the Copy Department was still called the Literary Department – a hangover from the time in the Twenties when Bobby Bevan and Dorothy Sayers were writing the ads (and she was writing *Murder Must Advertise*). In 1938 or thereabouts Stanley Penn had already composed his masterly Guinness poster:

> If he can say as you can
> 'Guinness is good for you'
> How grand to be a toucan!
> Just think what two can do.

This is light verse of a very high standard – though it did owe a lot to the drawing. We were told, as part of the advertising mystique, that 'two' was as far as you could go. Beyond that, you would be encouraging drunkenness. John Chenevix-Trench was the other Guinness copywriter. He wrote extremely witty and competent parodies of Lewis Carroll for the doctors, invoked as the greatest supporters of the divine liquid. These parody-pamphlets enjoyed free distribution to the medical profession; Guinness, I think, was also provided free in hospitals, for nursing mothers.

Byron himself at one time wrote advertising verse, in honour of Warren's Blacking (used for polishing boots). Mrs Warren, head of the firm, was very proud of this. 'We employs a poet!' was her confident boast. The actual verse is disappointing – not up to the standard of *Don Juan*.

Another area of ordinary life that is still not untouched by poetry is sport. Ian Hamilton once ran a feature in *New Review* entirely devoted to the songs sung by Chelsea fans at football matches, in which the opposition are untiringly portrayed as wankers. The standard of this verse was not high. Rugger songs, on the contrary, though more (or at least equally) obscene, have often some literary merit: 'If I were a marrying girl, which thank the Lord I'm not, Sir,/ I'd rather marry a scrum half than any other man I know!/ Oh! I'd put it in, he'd put it in, we'd put it in together!/ It'd be all right in the middle of the night, putting it in together'. The other positions featured are a full back ('I'd find touch, he'd find touch, we'd find touch together!'), a forward ('I'd push hard, he'd push hard, we'd push hard together!') and there's a reference to tackling ('I'd go low, he'd go low, we'd go low together'). Different versions exist, but it's fairly clear that this is the ghost of an Eighteenth Century drinking song adapted to modern conditions. This is the highbrow end of bawdy verse, where no obscene words are used. There's one famous one, where Keble College, Oxford, can be inserted at will, as a No Go area for hedgehogs:

> The exhaustive and careful enquiries
> Of Darwin and Huxley and Ball
> Have conclusively proved that the Hedgehog
> Can hardly be buggered at all –
> But further most painful researches
> Have incontrovertibly shown
> That this state of comparative safety
> Is enjoyed by the Hedgehog alone.

Popular songs, from the sophisticated works of Cole Porter to the more demotic lyrics of the Beatles, have always had a lot in common with 'respectable' poetry; and this is true of tabloid journalism too. As one of the Grimm brothers wrote of the fairy tales of folklore: *Das volk dichtet* – the people writes poetry.

FORTHCOMING ...

Summer issue:
LIVES OF THE POETS II
Biographies of Baudelaire, Mallarmé, Kipling, Hardy, Tennyson, and Eliot.
And > Serious Play Syndrome: Miroslav Holub interviewed > John Bayley on Douglas Dunn > E.A. Markham on Caribbean Poetry > Conor Kelly on Ciaron Carson > Ken Smith on the Poetry of Conflict > Helen Dunmore on Carol Rumens > Plus poems by Tom Paulin, Peter Redgrove, Michael Longley, Maureen Wilkinson, Stephen Smith, Martin Mooney, Wendy Cope, Sujata Bhatt.

Autumn issue:
NEW AGE CLASSICS
There's been a huge revival of interest in the classics recently. Heaney, Longley, Lasdun, Mahon, Hofmann, and Ellis have all produced versions ...

PAULINE STAINER
Sighting the Slave Ship

PAULINE STAINER WAS BORN IN STOKE-ON-TRENT IN 1941. SHE WAS AWARDED A HAWTHORNDEN Fellowship in 1987, and two years later produced her first collection, *The Honeycomb* (Bloodaxe). *Sighting the Slave Ship* was published in 1992 by Bloodaxe, who will also publish her next volume, *The Ice-Pilot Speaks*, later this year.

'We came to unexpected latitudes' runs the first line of *Sighting the Slave Ship*'s title poem – a sentence which accurately announces Stainer's style and concerns. A sense of spiritual adventure pervades her work, sustained by a poetic language that is strangely prescient. Typically she prefers to view life via works of art, especially paintings. 'Paul Klee at Pompeii, 1902' describes how the artist 'tilted/magic squares/into impulses of grief', detailing the dilemma of being 'caught between polarities'. Pain and beauty are two popular poles, as in 'St Sebastian' where the saint's sado-masochistic ecstasy is both enjoyed – 'His body is juiced sweeter/than any girl's' – and questioned: 'How should we read/such carnal knowledge/as the wounds whistle by?' The balancing act of art and life is reattempted in 'Cocteau as Equilibrist'; unfashionably, Stainer's titles tend to signpost her thematic territory: 'Equipping the Spirit', 'Structuring the Silence' and, best of all, 'Music for Invasive Surgery'. The grand claim that Stainer is seeking to redefine the *sacred* in the light of modern scientific investigations and modernist art experimentation is not entirely without substance. Certainly in her best work she fuses intellect and intuition, her words acting as 'exotic particles', bouncing off and blurring into one another. It is this which makes Stainer a (perhaps surprisingly) up-to-the-minute writer, distinctively post-religious. Poetically, her depth of perception can result in remarkable imagery: her fine 'Modern Angels' sequence, almost harrowing in the unswervingness of its vision yet at the same time clearly compassionate, shows the poet as precise mystic. In the long title sequence of *The Ice-Pilot Speaks* the limits of physical and mental endurance are tested in *terra incognita* – it's a disturbing depiction of the soul's long dark night set in sub-zero temperature. Stainer is too esoteric for some, but her seriousness is beyond doubt and her poetry is attracting increasingly rapt attention. **(KJ)**

Pauline Stainer writes:
(A page from the 'scribbling book'. It's my source of dangerous constancy – all that I read, or experience, or think about, gets distilled onto the chaotic little pages. It shows the electrical impulses behind the poems.)

The flash from the scree – flints igniting ... The *visceral* Muse – merciless innocence of the child's eye – Magritte's 'treachery of images' ... The discipline with which you use dissonance – as in the final aria of Monteverdi's *Coronation of Poppaea* ... 'Exotic couplings' – the strange attractor – sub-atomic particles that carry

with them 'chaotic and unpredictable evolution' – 'a crucial source of variability' ...

Gossamer slung between furrows – I was driving between ploughed fields – small furrows – *only* if you looked directly into the sun could you see Infinite Gossamers–slung between the ridges – all moving and shimmering – you couldn't see them if you looked obliquely ... Axes of vision ... Seeing without the eye.

Three influential 20th C. books:
In Parenthesis, David Jones; *Tenebrae*, Geoffrey Hill; *Collected Poems*, Robert Graves.

THREE POEMS BY PAULINE STAINER

Gilgamesh

In the mountain pass
he watched the lions play
by moonlight

their manes electric-blue,
the stars percussionists
through the frost.

Raging, he tore them
limb from limb,
ripped out their hearts.

Years later
they rose up before him
in the underworld

shook their manes
like shining turbines
through the updraught

until the fever-blisters
broke out on his lip —
and remembering

the hanging fire
of their wounds,
he felt again

the strange *rubato*
of his own heart
beating with theirs

for several minutes
after extraction.

Onnagata

The stage is white as a soda plain,
the kabuki actors
sashed with cinnabar.

Autumn ties its bloodknot;
circular jades
swing through the upper snow.

Between dancer and instrumentalist
the onnagata plays
a young girl returning

in the spirit of a heron,
his face so thickly powdered,
nothing can mask

the way his mouth
searches her breast
beneath the processional silks.

Beardsley at Dieppe

His hectic dust
haunts the casino;
he would come when
the tables were deserted,
the gambling rooms empty,
looking for something frivolous
in the presence
of abstracts.

It still intoxicates –
absinthe greening the sun
in an offshore wind,
the hot sweet haemorrhage
as on the dolorous page
Isolde drains
the scarlet philtre
from her glass.

The Radiant Sign

Pauline Stainer considers the affirming artistry of David Jones – poet, novelist, painter and maker of meaning

Selected Works of David Jones,
Ed. John Matthias,
National Poetry Foundation, Maine (USA)
& University of Wales Press, £10.95,
ISBN 0 7083 11695

I t wasn't gradual dazzle. When I went to the Tate exhibition of David Jones' work in 1981 I was stunned by a series of watercolours that included 'Flora in Calix-light'. These paintings of glass vessels on a table in front of his window at Harrow were luminous to an extraordinary degree – tangled cups of radiance, braided wounds, healing backlit. I had known other drawings of his and been fascinated by their scumbles and reworkings; I had stumbled through the poems, fought the thickets of notes. I still do. I had been haunted by his Christian legionaries in Jerusalem when I saw the Roman steps lead down from the High Priest's house. I had come upon the 'living lettering' of his inscriptions textured with wax and chalk, and later on Chinese white. They had seemed to me to catch exactly, that 'rubato' which Barthes defines as the 'theft of the object for the sake of the attribute'. But it was the watercolours of chalice and sweetbriar that became what Coleridge calls 'a Species of Revelation'.

And so I returned to the poetry with eyes unseeled. I disinterred the Sleeping Lord whose body is his own slumbering land. I saw the diversity of the things 'laid up from other things' – the magical allusiveness – the strata of Celtic and classical, 'Electra chose / from the seven stars in the sky'. David Jones didn't consider himself a scholar – 'It's not a matter of knowledge but of love' – but as Peter Levi says, he knew the point where the world 'runs backward into its origins'. It was this that gave such quality to his re-imagining. The 'historic provenance' of the word, the 'inward continuity of site' were indistinguishable; the Roman wolf suckles the Agnus Dei; the Annunciation takes place in a Welsh hill setting; the angel wears the saps of the stigmata. And as a poet, I responded to the way he used imagery, his belief

that 'images used are meant to mean as much as you can make them mean'; the Lady of the Pool as a 'waterside tart of sorts', a woman, a lavender-seller, a goddess. The flexing of his watercolours, the 'bright counter-rhythms of the water-brooks' in the Black Mountains, spring from the same marvellously unsystematic imagination. Tristan, aboard ship and about to sail, releases his falcon into the salt headwind against the golden squall of Isolde's hair.

It was fun too – this improvising, this arsing about with words, 'the process almost identical to what one tries to do in paintin' and drawin'.' The sharp reversals reminded me of Lear's fool. What kind of flip-somersault was it, that made David Jones take a phrase from Lewis Carroll's *The Hunting of the Snark*, 'the five unmistakeable marks' to evoke Christ's wounds in No-Man's Land? These 'queer reboundings' amazed me with their daring: the Corpus Christi carol in the trenches –

No one sings: Lully lully
for the mate whose blood runs down

– a nursery rhyme for the sexual tension of the Virgin seen as both mother and lover –

Such was her bread and honey
When his darling Body (of her body)
he won Tartary.

It seems unfashionable in the late twentieth century to claim as David Jones does, that the 'artist has both to believe and to tremble and somehow or other to affirm delight'. But how do we deal with the fact that we are 'wounded of necessity' unless it is by seeking to find 'formal goodness in a life singularly inimical, hateful to us'? When David Jones speaks of 'the bugger of' using the imagination to transubstantiate, he recalls Hopkins' 'Pitched past pitch of grief', the strange pressure on the artist to hold suffering to the light. In *In Parenthesis* it is the rats who 'redeem the time of our uncharity' with their own paradise.

Like Lancelot Andrewes, David Jones strikes a 'tally between the *Signe* and the *Signatum*'. The Mass is a 'making other', the raid on the inarticulate is to find signs 'radiant with otherness'. This affirmation, this determining to see art as a reaching prism, is something we are now oddly reluctant to acknowledge. The stream of consciousness rarely includes the sacramental. But I believe even Beckett's 'No bones but say bones' in *Worstward Ho* stems from the same mysterious 'drive to other and more radiant affinities'. Why else make the shape with words?

Of all the 'things that are signs of something', David Jones' *A, a, a, Domine Deus* touches me the most. As we approach the millennium, we increasingly 'liquidate the holy diversities'. The bombardment of the media results paradoxically in the erosion of signs: 'the sweet remembered demarcations / wither / to the touch of us'. Wordsworth had looked forward to that moment when science would put on flesh and blood in the words of poets. But David Jones speaks of feeling in desperation 'for His Wounds / in nozzles and containers' at the turn of a civilisation; and asks perhaps more pertinently than any other writer this century, how 'we shall enoble our new media as we have already ennobled and made significant our old'.

In his requiem sermon for David Jones, Peter Levi spoke of man as a sacramental creature: 'We are creatures, our service and our remembrance are creaturely. We kiss the cloth on the altar. We shall all die'. This creatureliness, what Jeremy Hooker calls 'a Franciscan tenderness' informs all David Jones' work. In *The Sleeping Lord*, water is 'the patient creature'; in the Preface to *In Parenthesis*, technology spawns 'creatures of chemicals'. Jones' comrades in his battalion of the Royal Welch Fusiliers are loved above all, as *creatures*: 'These were the children of Doll Tearsheet. Those are before Caractacus was'. The magical equity of the Queen of the Woods is to bring bright boughs to each dead soldier according not to rank, but to innate valour. It is almost Spenserian – this specific gravity of the blood.

Read John Matthias' marvellous selection, with its winnowed notes; read this 'heap of all I could find'. David Jones believed the task of the artist was to lift up creaturely signs. He called it simply 'a writing'. But how it bleeds for all those who lie with steel bolts through their breasts in the marketplace at Sarajevo ...

> You ought to ask: Why,
> what is this,
> what's the meaning of this.
> Because you don't ask,
> although the spear-shaft
> drips,
> there's neither steading – not a roof-tree.

MONIZA ALVI
The Country at my Shoulder

MONIZA ALVI WAS BORN IN LAHORE IN 1954 AND MOVED TO ENGLAND AT AN EARLY AGE. SHE CO-EDITED *Poetry London Newsletter* for two years. She was joint winner of the Poetry Business Competition in 1991 and her pamphlet, *Peacock Luggage* (with David Morley) was published by Smith/ Doorstop in 1992. *The Country At My Shoulder* (Oxford Poets), her first full collection, was a Poetry Book Society Recommendation and was shortlisted for the T. S. Eliot Prize. It is reviewed by Linda France on page 90.

Moniza Alvi has developed a subtle technique of writing in a light (in Calvino's sense), fantastical way which allows a deeper meaning to emerge without labouring the point. 'I want to be a dot in a painting by Miro' is the best known example (see comments by children on pages 96-7 and politicians on pages 38-9). The transformations that occur in her poems are often Chagalesque. 'The Great Pudding' – blended in a mixer lorry and delivered to the Town Hall – is an emblem of civic health: 'the dark moist heart/ when fruit hugs fruit'. 'Houdini', printed here, portrays the male in sex as an escapologist. Superficially more straightforward, her poems about her Pakistani background are not quite what they seem because until recently Pakistan too was a fantasy – she left the country as a young child. So the gorgeousness of spices and saris is freighted with longing. 'The Draught', full of details concerning wearing shawls over salwar kameez against the cold, becomes explicit at one point: 'And the draught?/ The great draught/ blowing me/ to my the birthplace ...' If she can truly fuse her allegorical inventions with her investigations into her background she will have achieved something very special. **(PF)**

Moniza Alvi writes:
Through the writing of my first full-length collection, *The Country at my Shoulder*, I was able to introduce the possibility of returning in my actual life to my birthplace, Pakistan, which I left when a few months old. Currently I am working on a group of poems centred on that first return visit and my impressions of family and country. Some of the poems are primarily concerned with practical social and personal detail while others, for instance 'The Wedding', seek to combine this with a more mysterious level of writing. The points where East and West converge are as crucial as they were in my earlier work, but in a less directly autobiographical sense. The poems which do not concern my Asian background are equally important to me. When I started writing seriously – about nine years ago – I was reading Angela Carter's work and J. G. Ballard's science fiction. I am attracted by

the strange-seeming and by fantasy, and find there some essence of experience. I consider my work with young people as a comprehensive school teacher helpful in keeping alive the creative impetus, but it doesn't leave much time for writing, so I'm planning to teach part-time next year.

Three influential 20th C. books:
I find it difficult to say who's influenced me, but the following books have certainly made a strong impression on me: Edward Thomas, *Collected Poems*, Jacques Prèvert, *Paroles*, Stevie Smith, *Selected Poems*.
Do you feel a special affinity towards any of your contemporaries?
I do feel an affinity with poets from a multi-cultural background, or those that have a multiracial identity, eg Mimi Khalvati and Sujata Bhatt.

THREE POEMS BY MONIZA ALVI

Houdini

It is not clear how he entered me
or why he always has to escape.
Maybe he's just proving to the crowds
he can still do it – He whispers
half-words which bloom in the dark
Ma ha ma ha.

Sometimes he feeds me cough medicine.
Or bathes his genitals in salt water.
Then heaves his body upwards
as if pressing against a lid.
At least he prefers me
to his underwater box, to the manacles
which clank on his moon-white skin.
I wonder what it is exactly
he sees within me?
He touches my insides as though
he'd sighted the first landplants –
I'm catching cloud between my fingers.

Tonight the wind whips through my stomach
over knots of trees and sharp rocks.
When he rushes out of me the crowd gasps –
and I implode from sheer emptiness.

Hindi Urdu Bol Chaal

These are languages I try to touch
as if my tongue is a fingertip gently
matching its whorls to echoings of sound.

Separating Urdu from Hindi – it's like
sifting grains of wild rice
or separating India from Pakistan.

The sign of nasal intonation
floats like a heat haze
above new words.

Words like hands banging on the table.

*

I introduce myself to two languages,
but there are so many – of costume,
of conduct and courtesy.

I listen hard as if to sense minute
changes of dialect from village to village
from West Punjab to West Bengal.

These languages could have been mine –
the whisper of silks on silks
and the slapping and patting of chapattis
on the tava.

*

I imagine the meetings and greetings
in Urdu borrowed from Sanskrit,
Arabic and Persian.

I shall be borrowed from England.
Pakistan, assalaam alaikum –
Peace be with you – Helloji.

It is not you I am meeting.
It is a sound system travelling through
countries, ascending and descending

in ragas, drumbeats, clapping.

*

In Lahore there grows a language tree
its roots branching to an earlier time
its fruit ripe, ready to fall.

I hear the rustling of mango groves
my living and dead relatives
quarrelling together and I search

for a nugget of sound, the kernel
of language. I am enlarged
by what I cannot hear –

the village conferences, the crackling
of bonfires and the rap of gunfire.

*

My senses stir with words
that must be reinvented.
At the market I'll ask *How much?*

and wait for just one new word
to settle like a stone
at the bottom of a well.

(Bol Chaal – dialogue)*

The Wedding

I expected a quiet wedding
high above a lost city
a marriage to balance on my head

like a forest of sticks, a pot of water.
The ceremony tasted of nothing
had little colour – guests arrived

stealthy as sandalwood smugglers.
When they opened their suitcases
England spilled out.

They scratched at my veil
like beggars on a car window.
I insisted my dowry was simple –

a smile, a shadow, a whisper,
my house an incredible structure
of stiffened rags and bamboo.

We travelled along roads with English

names, my bridegroom and I.
Our eyes changed colour

like traffic-lights, so they said.
The time was not ripe
for us to view each other.

We stared straight ahead as if
we could see through mountains
breathe life into new cities.

I wanted to marry a country
take up a river for a veil
sing in the Jinnah gardens,

hold up my dream, tricky
as a snake-charmer's snake.
Our thoughts half-submerged

like buffaloes under dark water
we turned and faced each other
with turbulence

and imprints like maps on our hands.

Unravelling a Sari

by Linda France

Moniza Alvi,
The Country at my Shoulder,
Oxford Poets, £6.99,
ISBN 0 19 283125 9

As its title suggests, Moniza Alvi's first collection, *The Country at my Shoulder*, balances the autobiographical and the elemental, the emotional and the physical, in a wide variety of poems that are at once relaxed and authoritative. The interplay of her various angles and levels evokes a world where East is superimposed upon West, seeing upon believing, the elevated upon the earthy, and the poems conspire to make a map of this

> country at my shoulder,
> growing larger – soon it will burst,
> rivers will out, run down my chest.

Many are written through the eyes of childhood, graphically creating a personal mythology out of experience, memory and anecdote. But Alvi also writes with her body, recording perception directly via the physical. This poetry is deceptively simple, disarmingly truthful, full of a vivid and delicate individuality and *jouissance*. She creates her own version of herself, weaving together the threads of her birth in Pakistan and her upbringing in England, displaying a fine tension between containment and expansiveness. The connection with her birthplace is maintained and unravelled in the central section 'Presents from Pakistan', contributing to the richness and intricacy of her story.

There is often a sensual and emotional recollection of setting and weather, nature perceived and portrayed as truly natural; also a strong fascination for the childhood taboos of turds, death and family fights, reflected in a keen visual sense. What she sees is what she feels and vice versa. Here is a small child looking at the world in the same way an adult would look at a painting. In fact Alvi inhabits this very viewpoint in 'I'd Like to be a Dot in a Painting by Miro', a playful and intelligent fantasy. Her imagination is always exotic and nimble, with the consist-

ent and satisfying depth of an articulate emotional source: Alvi is clever enough to know it's not enough to be clever. What is exciting here is where she chooses to stand in relation to the themes of her poems: the effect is that she seems tucked away in a corner and smack bang in the centre at the same time: 'And nothing in this tawny sky / can get too close, or move too far away'.

As well as focusing upon the body, the physical, Alvi often looks at clothing as suggestive of the cultural and psychological layers accrued in a lifetime:

> All the people unravelled a sari.
> It stretched from Lahore to Hyderabad,
>
> ...
>
> Eventually
> they wrapped me in it
> whispering *Your body is your country.*

In this way she conveys the pull towards and the tug away from a geographical/cultural definition of herself. Whilst honouring the importance of her heritage, Alvi also seems to be striving to discover who she is apart from that; the issue of nature versus nurture dramatically manifest in her history and experience.

A western garment Alvi uses in more than one poem as a vehicle to convey thoughts and feelings about selfhood is the glove. 'I Was Raised in a Glove Compartment' reveals 'I existed in the quiet – I listened / for the sound of the engine'. Gloves appear as warmth and the possibility of protection, provided by distance, a necessary 'layer between' to soften anxiety, vulnerability, feelings of displacement. Alongside the sense of her capacity for luxuriating surrender, there is also the awareness of danger, felt even by the braid of hair kept wrapped in newspaper, and fever, like the heat of chillies; then there's the modern dictionary, unlike her father's, with words such as *chador* and *sick building syndrome*, that she can't bring herself to inscribe her name in.

This mixture of delight and darkness 'where chaos and enchantment / jostle like relatives' is more overtly addressed in several mythic fairy tale pieces, like 'Red Ridinghood's Plan' and 'The Great Pudding', as well as her own narratives of quests and dreams, 'The Fire-Walk', 'The Air Was Full of Starfish' and 'The Bed', with its wished-for river in the middle 'Where in the ancient song / the King's horses could all drink together'. The key, as in all myths and fairy stories, is transformation, the alchemist's art, which lies at the heart of this accomplished collection.

GLYN MAXWELL
Out of the Rain

GLYN MAXWELL WAS BORN IN 1962 IN WELWYN GARDEN CITY WHERE HE STILL LIVES. HE PUBLISHED his first poem, in *Poetry Review*, in 1986. In 1987 he studied on Derek Walcott's Writing Program at Boston. He has published poems and reviews consistently in *Poetry Review* and was featured in the 'New British Poets' issue in 1987. Maxwell's first book, *Tale of the Mayor's Son* (Bloodaxe, 1990) was a Poetry Book Society Choice. *Out of the Rain* was published by Bloodaxe in 1992 and reviewed by David Kennedy in *Poetry Review*, Autumn 1992. Maxwell has won many awards, including a Somerset Maugham Award. In 1992 he produced his verse play *The Birthday Ball of Zelda Nein* in his garden; *Gneiss the Magnificent* followed in 1993 and three plays were published by Chatto in *Gneiss the Magnificent*, 1993. *Blue Burneau*, a novel, is published by Chatto in June.

Maxwell began with a remarkably developed formal facility and an extreme evasiveness with subject matter. Where Frost, one of his heroes, played the sound of sense over the patterns of metre, Maxwell played the sounds of syntax, of linguistic counters, vernacular tics, fairy tales and grotesqueries over that same metrical grid. The result was a bit like Auden's first book, compelling through its sheer linguistic élan, but sometimes lacking the recognizable human moods we look for in poetry. Despite this, there are many poems that catch recognizable aspects of the 80s: 'Just Like Us' (sympathetic and humane treatment of our yen for soap opera), 'The End of the Weekend' (the void at the heart of the consumer weekend), 'Sports Story of a Winner' (the tabloid epic of football), 'Helen and Heloise' (gels disporting beside a pool), 'We Billion Cheered' (passivity in the face of media-managed news). The long Noah's Ark dramatic poem entitled 'Out of the Rain', for all its Welwyn lager-loutishness (actually they drink manzadinkas), is reminiscent of Wallace Stevens in its constant conjuring of suggestive music. He has written well about Bosnia, and his style seems capable of addressing great public issues. **(PF)**

Glyn Maxwell writes:
Perhaps my days of rôle-playing idiosyncratically sly or stupid citizens wandering around shouting are drawing to a close. If true, this is because all those characters have decamped *en masse* towards a darkened theatre where they wait to be auditioned for the verse-plays to which I mean to devote the years to come, and which in my opinion are more interesting and rewarding than anything else I've assembled. The poem 'Tale of the Mayor's Son' has been cut from line 4 to the end. By and large this development seems to be leaving me – in the poems – with a quieter, briefer voice that speaks both more intelligently and more intelligibly about things quite personal to me, even things that actually happened. I have so far spoken only three or four times with this voice, but I recognize it as both truer and therefore stronger. Everything else, everything hitherto, is a sort of light display powered by manifold sources – delight in English, delight in form, delight in Auden and Frost; fortune in my family circumstances, fortune in the acquaintance of fine poets; complete ignorance of and independence from all movements, schools, ideas and theories; wanting to impress, wanting to be liked, wanting to make a living making myself happy. I am.

Three Influential 20th C. Books:
W. H. Auden, *Selected Poems*; Robert Frost, *Selected Poems*; Bob Dylan, early music of, would have to come before any books.

TWO POEMS BY GLYN MAXWELL
Points of Compass

Above the Brandenburg Gate there is a quadriga
Of galloping horses and these have been galloping either
East or west for years but without of course
Reaching a point. They have crumpled and flared in wars.
Thirteen more gates, the Wall to the north and south:

History. I could see, from far above,
The lonely Gate as I sat in the heavenly suite,
Revolving over Berlin. My eyes and mouth
Would face in an hour all ways. I could watch and eat
Everything, make doing that enough.

To the West
In are the sweet, the welcome flavours, in
Melt the appealing, the textured soften, all
Decreasing to luck, to the tiny sugary tide
Below one blissful tongue, that licks like a whole
Cat. The mouth is empty and satisfied.

A carious molar rocks at the brink of there.
Under and either side it is riddled with pain.
Love has done this, blurt the appalled insides,
Shutting their lips on air. When they part again
It will be to binge, alone, not telling where.

To the South
The thinner the meal, the keener the eye. At least
Up to the death of the flyblown black and starved
Among the swollen this is the case. But I loved
It getting so hot in school we sat on the field
To hear a story, listen, dream and be lost . . .

Teacher shushes an Africa with the one
Final chapter, closes the book and sighs
Her sound for pleasure. This many bulging eyes
Can no more hear than eat. This story's old.
She asked for questions. Suddenly there were none.

To the East
'The opposite is not the case.' This is how
We worked and how we turned the rivers brown,
Glassed the desert, dropped diarrhoetic loads,
Scythed or stripped or otherwise went to mow.
We were the toads that hated the other toads

For how they croaked. We were the A to M,
Sworn to destroy the N to Z. On the day
The Z comes we will mash our dwellings in
Sooner than say it. Come the Millennium,
'The opposite is not the case', we will say.

TO THE NORTH
The polar dumb and the luckless we will save
As we look out, the pines and the languages
Spoken in huddles, the likelihood of riches
Under the floes, the distances of love,
The cosiness of the cuddled-up against night,

Good people in their element, essentials
By their huts, the fabulous solar light!
– Thus the unquiet races lift their eyes
Beyond the northernness of all night skies
Towards the corroboration of the angels.

TO THE WEST AND HOME
Then I was facing the way I faced when I
Was hungry and knew nothing of this town.
Now I am full and even the Queen has come
Progressing under the archway under the eye
Of Europe. We will both be where we come from

Christmas Day: both of us will sit down
To talk like the young of a land where there are no lost.
Snow will melt on the manes of the copper horses
In neither East nor West Berlin and their faces
Will stare at us and beyond us, like the past.

Morning Going Now

There is this mystical congress
    behind suburban houses,
or has been while I've been here
    or while as a child I *was* here.
You wonder how so private
    a view can be so public.
You wonder why we don't just
    forget the streets and traffic
and saunter up and meet there,
    discuss what might be happening
this evening in our houses.
    And once of course we did do.

Once we made a lamp shine
    across three lawns of airspace
towards a pal's back window:
    he shone his own towards us.
His blue light to our red light,
    our violet to his yellow,
this was a holy nattering
    in infinite dizzy nighttime.
Something to remember:
    a silent beam of colour
that meant no less than 'morning'
    or 'going now' or 'question'.

The professorial present
cannot recall exactly
the meaning of the structure,
but only look with certainty
across three lawns of airspace,
between the stars and hedges,
for absences of adults
behind suburban houses,
and feel an ancient, frozen want
of friends in back windows,
to make a shining language with
and use it when you have to.

Calypso: A Caribbean Tale

Glyn Maxwell fulfils the terms of his Somerset Maugham Travel Prize in the West Indies

The British West Indian Airlines in-flight magazine was extremely illuminating. I learned from the quiz at the back, as we failed to make out the Azores somewhere to our right, that the Nobel Prize-winning poet born in St Lucia was called Derek Walcot, while my travelling companion, the theatre director Greg Doran, was interested to discover that this 'Walcot' wrote his version of *The Odyssey* for the National Theatre, since Greg distinctly remembered directing it for the RSC. Still, there it was in print, and print is what we live by, so we sat back among the holidaymakers, returning exiles and masochistic English cricket fans, and contemplated ten days of unstinting hedonism in temperatures 30 degrees higher than Heathrow.

Is it only creative types who go on holiday regarding everyone else as a holidaymaker? Probably, because we can't conceive of what it is to take time off, or we believe that the laziest days and mellowest nights can be somehow pressed into the service of what we call work. But we did have work to do. Greg, after all, had half his fare paid by the Trinidad Theatre Workshop, for whom he is to direct Walcott's *The Joker of Seville* this summer, and he was flying out to hold auditions and cast the play. I, meanwhile, courtesy of the largesse of the Society of Authors, was merely fulfilling the terms of the Somerset Maugham Travel Prize: put on a panama hat and go away. If my horizon-broadening work demanded that I sit in the garden of the Walcott residence sipping rum and watching hummingbirds at the hibiscus, or fireflies come out like stars, just as in the

man's poem, then so be it. It just so happened that Greg's auditioning and my, well, observing, coincided with what is generally thought to be the world's biggest, longest and loudest party: the Trinidad Carnival. Forget Rio, forget Notting Hill, this is days and nights of parties, balls and parades, fuelled by rum and calypso, roti and steel bands, played in masks and greasepaint and fabulous costumes, virtually unpoliced, and virtually – with the exception of an inebriated British journalist I had to extricate from a fight – trouble-free.

Greg approached Carnival with a mysterious sense of responsibility. It was he who commissioned Derek to write a new verse play of *The Odyssey* which, during its run at Stratford and the Barbican, was also given a staged reading by the Trinidad Theatre Workshop in Port of Spain. This had planted Homeric thoughts in the mind of one Peter Minshall, a designer whose genius and ambition are almost legendary in the world of Carnival (and outside: his commissions include the opening ceremony of the Barcelona Olympics) and who set about designing two dozen costumes depicting the adventures of Odysseus, as a theme for his 'band'. A band in Carnival terms means several thousand people who parade (or 'play') together, having shelled out some £60 for the privilege of wearing a costume. Minshall's band is an annual institution: outrageous costumes, beautiful tottering puppets five times higher than the person inside them, and always the likelihood of something collapsing in spectacular fashion, as nothing made in Minshall's factory (or mas' camp) is ever ready on time. He did not disappoint.

Margaret Walcott, at whose house we were staying, played in Minshall's 'Odyssey' as one of Circe's Swine. Since the Swine, along with the Drowned Sailors, the Laestrygonians, Rape and Pillage I and Rape and Pillage II, were fully booked by the time we arrived, Greg and I considered playing as two Sheep of the Cyclops, but decided in the end that we had more to fear from the one eye of the Caribbean sun and opted for the shady sidelines, occasionally taking cups of rum to the perspiring Swine. There were certainly times, as a seemingly endless procession of Penelope's Maidens crossed Port of Spain while we wilted in the upper twenties, when I thought of asking Greg why the RSC couldn't have commissioned *The Wanderer* or *The Seafarer* from Derek, something slightly more austere, but I'm not one to give a man dangerous ideas.

Anyway, the Carnival itself passed off in a blaze of, well, in a blaze, from my being woken at 2 a.m. on Monday morning by Margaret asking 'Do you all want rum, scotch or gin in your bottles?' so we could join in the celebration of J'Ouvert ('le jour est ouvert') – essentially dancing half-naked and smeared in mud through Port of Spain to watch the sunrise – to flaking out at the far end of Tuesday, as the last of Penelope's Maidens wandered unsteadily into the dusk, and the Society of Authors will be pleased to know that I have it all somewhere in my head.

Derek had flown to St Lucia for some peace and quiet, once he and Greg had cast the play. The audition was an opportunity to see (if not hear: a steel band was doing its stuff outside) the workings of the Trinidad Theatre Workshop, founded by Derek thirty years ago. The company is a blend of professionals and generally gifted amateurs, old stagers and new talents; Walcott plays form the bulk of their repertoire. Of course, just as this group is spearheading a general flowering of theatrical endeavour on Trinidad, by performing the works of a globally renowned poet, the Government, which is unpopular with the creative and appears to depend for its power upon the self-interested and the uneducated – sound familiar? – is trying to kick them out of their premises, a wonderful decayed old fire station right across the street from the Red House, Trinidad's Parliament. Indeed, the theatre is so literally close to the heart of power that during the bizarre Islamic coup attempt of 1990, shots were fired into the theatre's roof as the actors rehearsed. Anyway, the Government wants a Central Library, not a lively theatre, though there seems little demand for bookshops on the island.

The most important and passionately discussed element of Trinidad at Carnival time is not theatre or poetry or costume design, however, but calypso. Far from being the grass-skirted gyration we associate with coconuts and Harry Belafonte, Trinidad calypso is purposeful folk music with a beat, folk song not as style or nostalgia but as genuine social comment. As the singers ('Calypsonians' with names like Shadow, Superblue, Lord Kitchener) compete annually for prizes at Carnival, a car, or money, or the chance to sing at Brooklyn or Toronto or Notting Hill, the relative merits of their songs are matters for serious debate. The Walcotts and their friends were especially disappointed that Shadow's hard-hitting 'Poverty is Hell' didn't make the final, and suggested that the judges were too timid to reward implicit criticism of the Government. (There is serious poverty in the hills above Port of Spain: squatters' shacks strewn haphazardly along dirt roads, all a painful contrast with the wealth of the 1970s oil boom, wealth widely felt to have been stupidly squandered.) Others, meanwhile, bemoaned the younger generation's voting with their dancing feet for songs that dispensed with politics and settled for the pleasures of 'Doing the Tidal Wave'.

But any matter that stirs a society across its generations while still representing at the very least a damn good time suggests a robust culture with a healthy sense of what's important and worth preserving. Trinidad, which, unlike Jamaica, has scarcely exported its music to the 'West', is resilient, too. No Michael Jackson, no Madonna, no Western rock music except toiletry commercials on the radio between calypsos. Coke and Kentucky Fried Chicken made it, but MacDonalds failed on Barbados and gave up. All this was a pleasant surprise to me, and it is perhaps a strength the Trinidadians rather take for granted.

The engagement of the artist with politics, with government, with social issues, is something I found inspiring. Trinidad is not yet a crime black spot – murders make the front page – and not yet entirely run by the professionally venal for the terminally fooled, but we have seen these things happen anywhere, and in one more country than Michael Portillo can think of, and the vigilance of the calypsonians, as well as those poets and playwrights who follow in the steps of Walcott or Brathwaite, is a credit to Trinidad. To consider the most popular music in contemporary Britain is to suffer a cringe more extreme and contorting than the one engendered by the comparison between a week of uninhibited, wild and essentially harmless pleasure and an afternoon spent running across a damp field tossing a pancake, which is how we let our hair down come Mardi Gras.

The Even Newer Generation

We sent a poem by each of the New Generation poets to several schools to get innocent eye reactions. The clear winner in terms of number of reactions was Moniza Alvi's 'I would like to be a dot in a painting by Miro'.

Moniza Alvi:
I would like to be a dot in a painting by Miro

I think Moniza trying to get across the fact that not everyone is noticed. It's like judging a book by its cover. In the line, 'People will stare forever', she means that finally she has become important.

Janine Adams, 13 (HMS)

I like the way that in every verse the dot gets more vain, until it decides that it's probably better where it is.

Catherine Cobb, 12 (HMS)

It seems the dot fancies the lemon stripe and it wants to be like the artist and survey the beauty of the linescape.

Tam Hamburger, 13 (HMS)

Elizabeth Garrett:
And the World in a Bowl of Porridge

It is quite realistic, especially the lines about playing with the porridge, which young children tend to do. The lines I like best are – 'The twisted ribbon of milk,/Round bouldered shores the white silk slips/And laps the island in,/Slowly the world revolves'. These lines describe a bowl of porridge turned into a world of islands and magic.

Hayley Brown, 12 (HMS)

Michael Hofmann:
From A to B and Back Again (see p. 49)

The music of the lines makes you want to read on. I can imagine everything the poet is saying. My favourite lines are the last:

> Like grappling hooks, one in the metropolis
> The other, some distance away, in the
>   unconcerned suburbs.

The poet was clever in writing those lines because it links with the 'cicatrice' of the railway tracks in the first verse.

Christine Land, 13 (HMS)

Glyn Maxwell: Song to the Skinhead

This poem is about a boy who was walking home from school one day and suddenly a skinhead rode past and yelled, 'Ginger you are going to die!' There is a boy in our class who has remarks made to him like that and when it was read out everybody looked at him! There is a piece near the end which was quite sarcastic. It reads:

> When I need to know
> that any can be loved, I do
> tend to begin with you.

Daniel Pearce, 12 (HMS)

Lavinia Greenlaw: River History

For hundreds of years the river has been used to transport cargo, treasures other people have discovered from the earth –

> cloves from Zanzibar, mother-of-pearl,
> tortoiseshell, South American iodine ...

This shows how people were willing to share their gifts with others. The poem progresses to show how people are becoming more selfish. On the whole, I think the poem is about how we abuse the world, slowly destroying it, and how self-centred people have become.

Lisa Shielly, 16 (RHS)

John Burnside: An Operating System

I was attracted to this poem because it could be true. You could discover an unexplored room or cave holding unknown secrets, tucked away in the basement past dad's gold clubs, round Mum's violin and at the end by chance you see a handle and move the shelves aside to investigate. But it could have a different meaning. It could be the unlocking of the deepest darkest secrets of your mind. My favourite lines are:

> like the wren's egg you find in a smokebush,
>   surprising and warm;

a thread in the fabric, and almost your only
clue.

This describes the secret of all secrets, the diamond
centrepiece in a crown of secrets.

Toby Dillaway, 12 (HMS)

Pauline Stainer:
Enclosed Wheatfield with Rising Sun

The reason I like this poem is that if Van Gogh had
been a poet he could have written it. The poem itself
is rather bizarre, the ending especially:

> The high white note
> of birds igniting
> in mid-air.

The idea of birds blowing up in mid-air could only
have been thought up by a sick mind. But yet there
is a strange beauty hidden in the words which sur-
passes all the thinking of such sane and logical
people as ourselves.

David Ribefors, 13 (HMS)

I particularly like the third verse which includes 'a
fire-ball in the mouth of a corpse', which I think is a
wonderful way of describing the sun rising.

Oscar Smith, 12 (HMS)

I really love the words about the sun:

> I whipped it
> until it cartwheeled like a sunflower

It brings visions of other Van Gogh paintings steaming back into life.

Joe Putnam, 13 (HMS)

Jamie McKendrick: Windrose (see p. 56)

(see p. 56)

A literary device the poet uses is to relate weather
with nature, eg 'windrose' and 'palm frond'. I feel
that the writer is hinting at something deeper than
the weather in this poem since he writes 'a pillar of
salt' which is obviously a reference to the Bible,
although I fail to decipher exactly what the real
meaning is.

Gillian Wilson, 16 (RHS)

Kathleen Jamie: China for Lovers

I found this poem amusing and touching. Through
its light, carefree, colloquial style the reader glimpses
small slices of Chinese life as seen by a tourist talking
to a lover. The atmosphere is built up by a series of
contrasts and combinations: passionate, heated un-
dertones with grim, ugly detail – 'noodle steam' with
'diesel', dirty poverty with affluent travellers.
Finally, despite the unhealthy staleness of the 'bus-
station motel' room, comes the vision of love's endurance, secret and alone.

Barbara Greenwood, 16 (HB)

Carol Ann Duffy: Prayer

I chose this poem not because it is by an award-
winning poet but because I think it says something
about what happens outside church, like where it
says:

> The truth
> enters our hearts, that small familiar pain

I think it simply means you are not telling the truth or
facing up to the truth. But the truth will still be there
and is not pleasant to hear. That is your pain.

Samantha Bassam, 13 (HMS)

Sarah Maguire: Mushrooms à la Grecque

It was about a love affair that ended the night before
for a reason we're not sure of. I felt the dampness in
the air from the steaming washing-up bowl and all
the misery of wiping over the dirty plates where the
Mushrooms à la Grecque had been.

Tanya Doughty, 13 (HMS)

I think she is saying the whole relationship is down
the drain.

Andrew Tyler, 13 (HMS)

**SCHOOLS: HMS (Halesworth Middle School,
Suffolk), HB (Henrietta Barnet School, North
London), RHS (Royal High School, Edinburgh).
Pupils of Halesworth Middle School have published a book of their own poems: Apple Fire,
edited by Jill Pirrie, Bloodaxe, £7.95. Apple Fire was
reviewed in Poetry Review, Winter, 1992/93.**

Poets visit schools under a Poetry Society
programme, the W.H. Smith Poets in Schools
scheme. For details, write to: Pel Plowden, Education Officer, The Poetry Society, 22 Betterton
Street, London WC2H 9BU.

MICK IMLAH
Birthmarks

MICK IMLAH WAS BORN IN ABERDEEN 1956 AND EDUCATED AT MAGDALEN COLLEGE, OXFORD. HE EDITED *Poetry Review* from 1983-6 and was Poetry Editor at Chatto from 1990-93. He now works part-time at the *TLS*. *Birthmarks* was published by Chatto in 1988 and reviewed by Martyn Crucefix in *Poetry Review*, Winter 1988-9.

Imlah's one book to date demonstrates his pedigree: Fenton and Fuller and behind it all, Browning. *The Zoologist's Bath*, the long poem that closes the book, is a quintessentially Oxonian work, concerning a Victorian eccentric, Arthur William Woolmer, who believed that the evolutionary fate of the human race is to return to the sea. This plot is no more than an excuse to indulge in the Browningesque. Imlah acknowledges that 'there is, relatively speaking an academic odour around some of my poems'. Elsewhere the technique is more modern. 'Jealousy' is a vicious poems whose quatrains could not have been written without the example of Fenton. Imlah's most impressive poem, 'Goldilocks', blends his Scottishness, Oxonian *hauteur*, and narrative flair, and delivers a neat moral: 'Note:/It uncovers a naked and difficult thought about beds,/Namely, that seldom again will there ever be one/With only you in it; take that however you will'. Imlah is an extremely formal poet, drawn to insidious feminine and trisyllabic rhymes: 'You offer me your hand? No damp on it?/Take back your hand before I stamp on it!'. He is even less prolific than Fenton and there seems to be a connection between the clenched formality they favour and the difficulty of writing. The new poem printed here shows even greater obsession with shape. **(PF)**

Mick Imlah writes:

Not long after I began, I became aware that what I seemed to write about were those things – class, family, congenital strengths and weaknesses, prejudices, addictions, tattoos, that people are stuck with, whether they like it or not. Of course this was a limitation as well as a discovery, but I accepted it, as a thing I was stuck with. And although my first book took about seven years to evolve, and though I tried to vary the forms and settings and colours of its parts, most of these answered in some way to its title – *Birthmarks*.

response to that possibility, I'm trying to find a more direct form of address, interspersing approaches to other lives with poems which come to terms with my own – but if I don't I'll only prove my point. Whatever, I'll be sticking to a belief that poems no less than prose fictions should somehow (whatever else they do) entertain or stimulate a reader, rather than exalting the writer. In this, humour can play a part, even in the most serious of poems.

After that book came out, I couldn't write poems for three or four years. When they started to come again, only about twelve months ago, it wasn't as individual poems so much as recognizable parts of another book, again about personal identity, but with a psychological focus where *Birthmarks* was broadly social. If *Birthmarks* says, we can only be what we are, this says, we can fail to be even that. In

Influential 20th C books?

I don't think any single book has influenced me particularly; like anyone I've absorbed things, consciously and unconsciously, from whatever I've read. My very first poems were reactions, as far as their form was concerned, to nineteenth-century models, but that was a long time ago.

MICK IMLAH

Past Caring

As a ship
Sees only the tip
Of the ice's pyramid
That has already scraped her bows,
We'd glimpsed that drink was something you overdid;
Now after the wreck I sift the damage you'd stowed in the house.

Eyes glazed
I fumble, amazed,
Through mounds of knickers and slips,
Extracting the bottles you'd buried there; these
I hump in their binbags, clashing against my knees
To the 'Bottlebank', by the public baths; it takes four trips.

The gin!
No wonder you're thin;
Hundreds of bottles of gin;
And feeding them singly into the ring
My arm grows weary from shifting the bottles of gin;
– A numbing collection of lots of exactly the same thing.

You were vain
As you went down the drain;
Why else would you lay up this hoard
If it wasn't one day to take stock as I'm doing
Of what an almighty amount you had taken on board?
And here am I turning your trophies to scrap at an illicit viewing!

A smear
of lipstick, here –
Like the kiss on a Valentine;
And sniffing the neck I feel suddenly dear to you,
For what it gives off is your smell, if we kissed anytime,
And it wasn't a cheap perfume – but the only thing properly dear to you.

Next week
If you're not past caring
They may let you out for an airing,
– To slump in your armchair, too burgled to speak,
The fish out of water that stubbornly stays but the more fish;
– Then how shall we drag the treasure you were back to the surface?

Tusking

In Africa once
A herd of Harrow
Elephants strayed
Far from their bunks;
Leather, they laid
Their costly trunks
And ears of felt
Down on the Veldt.

Out in the bush
Is silence now:
Savannah seas
Have islands now,
Smelly land-masses,
Bloody, cold,
Disfigured places
With fly-blown faces;

All forgot
The creep of dusk;
A moonbeam stole
Along each tusk:
Snores and sighs.
Oh, foolish boys!
The English elephant
Never lies!

And each of us rests
After his fashion:
Elephant, English,
Butcher, Bushman;
Now only the herding
Boy in a singlet
Worries his goat
With a peaceful prod.

*

*

In the night-time, lithe
Shadows with little
Glinting teeth
Whisked tusks away;
Drew through the dark
Branches of ivory,
Made a great hue
On their rapid run.

But if, one night
As you stroll the verandah
Observing with wonder
The place of the white
Stars in the universe,
Brilliant and clear,
Sipping your whisky
And pissed with fear

Hunters, at home
They curl up the bare
Soles of their feet
With piano-pleasure;
Sammy plays
A massacre song
With the notes wrong
On Massa's baby.

You happen to hear
Over the tinkle
Of ice and Schubert
A sawing - a drilling -
The bellow and trump
Of a vast pain -
Pity the hulks!
Play it again!

*

Reproduced from *Birthmarks*, by permission of Chatto

LAVINIA GREENLAW
Night Photograph

LAVINIA GREENLAW WAS BORN IN LONDON IN 1962 AND GREW UP IN ESSEX. SHE IS CURRENTLY Literature Officer at the London Arts Board. In 1990 she won a Gregory Award and was one of four poets chosen for the Poetry Society's 'Catch Words' tour. She has published two pamphlets – *The Cost of Getting Lost in Space* (Turret Books, 1991) and *Love from a Foreign City* (Slow Dancer, 1992) – and one full collection, *Night Photograph* (Faber, 1993), reviewed on page 104.

Lavinia Greenlaw's poetry engages fascinatingly with scientific subjects. On one level she is concerned with the 'decimal places' which demarcate the limits of knowledge, and the analogous 'molecular shifts' which constitute life-in-motion; on the other she is simply thrilled by the act of discovery. The 'exact miracle' which she writes about in 'Linear, Parallel, Constant' unites the scientific and artistic spheres and possesses a 'mathematical beauty' which periodically infiltrates ordinary life. *Night Photograph* is full of poems which enquire across geographical and/or historical boundaries. Sometimes, as in the charming 'Boris Goes Fishing', the boundary is language itself; at other times ('In the Zoo after Dark') the line questioned is between different species – 'Animals intended/to live an ocean apart/have got an idea of each other'. In Greenlaw's work the world is in a perpetual state of flux – 'The printing plates for the last atlas/were archived, unused', 'unexpected chemical reactions' are always occurring, subtly affecting the shape of things. Greenlaw's sensitivity to *change* is her finest quality, a poetic vigilance as to the delicate variance between one element and another. Her balance of theory and practice is at times precarious: in 'Suspension' she considers Brunel's famous bridge and contemplates 'the physics of what keeps us from falling'. The simultaneous acknowledgement of gravity and a dreamy desire to defy the natural laws are constants in her work. Often her poems end by enacting this conflict stylistically, lyrical release being promised but then withheld in favour of lucid documentary: 'There is a slight realignment of the planets,/day breaks at no particular moment'. **(KJ)**

Lavinia Greenlaw writes:
The Cost of Getting Lost in Space ...
My brother secretly borrowed a precious Schmidt Plate from his astrophysics lab. This is a photo of six degrees square of outer space taken with a high-resolution telescope. Even using one of the best lenses you can get, it is as grainy and vague as an old television screen after closedown. He pointed to a few of the white specks: 'There's a galaxy ... there's a galaxy ...' My head ached but I felt momentarily better about death.

and they happened to be listening to that particular station in his lab that afternoon. They were pleased to hear a poet writing about stars but he didn't get to borrow any more Schmidt Plates.

I don't know where poems come from. I spent a long time wandering around in outer space trying to make some sense of what goes on off the map, beyond the human scale, but also struggling with ways in which we make sense at all. Now I've moved back to within a mile of where I was born. I need more sleep.

The next night, he went to a party, fell asleep somewhere and mislaid the Plate. It surfaced eventually, and he returned it to the lab unnoticed. Then I went and wrote a poem about it. It got on the radio

Three influential 20th C. books:
Robert Lowell, *Life Studies*; Elizabeth Bishop, *Collected Poems*; Anna Akhmatova, *Rosary*.

THREE POEMS BY LAVINIA GREENLAW
Parallax

Joseph Banks and Captain Cook led an expedition to Tahiti, to observe the transit of Venus across the face of the sun in 1769. Parallax, or triangulation, is the method by which the distance of a planet from earth can be measured by the simultaneous observation of its position from two far separate points.

Halley left notes.
A dream of the triangle waiting to be drawn
from this occasional journey:

Venus crossing the face of the sun,
twice in a decade then not for a century.
Unseen by Halley who lived between.

                    *

The ship leaves Plymouth at the height of summer,
laden with barrels of the pickled cabbage
Cook swears will protect from scurvy.

Halley had prayed '. . . *that they not be deprived
. . . by the unfortunate obscuration of cloudy heavens . . .*'
Banks fills three cabins with telescopes and clocks.

                    *

Stomachs wrecked by sauerkraut, the officers order
a thousand gallons of wine at Madeira. Such skies!
It could be like reaching for a pebble

in a clear and shallow pond. No land in sight.
Anchored by the sun and stars. For months now,
the only map will be a cloudless night.

                    *

At the Falklands, a welcome from the Viceroy.
Banks demonstrates Harrison's marine chronometer.
Before this the pendulum had been confounded

by the roll of the waves. That night the Viceroy,
Unsettled by the Celtic hills and weather
that have followed him south,

dreams of scattered constellations, the slip of an axis,
wandering magnetic poles. As the ship moves out to sea,
he orders his troops to open fire.

*

Christmas in Tierra del Fuego.
The men celebrate on shore.
Banks' servants are lost in a snowstorm,

drunk, no sense of direction,
frozen to death.
It will be warmer in the west.

*

Buckets of nails to trade with the islanders.
The crew steal tools and cooking pots
for Tahitian women. Whispered stories

of tattoos on thighs, higher and higher.
Venus slides into focus.
Cook locks up all who try to desert.

Guidebooks to the Alhambra

Things change, become home and we must leave them.
What do you want? An untouchable sleep
in which I cannot touch you. This heat

opens my skin till I stare a reflection into beauty
and pull at your clothes. Do you remember that palace?
Where the rusted fountain was evidence

of the murder of the Abenceragas cavaliers.
One was found in the hollow trunk of a cypress
with the wife of Aben Hassan – or was it

Muley Abul Hassan, who had his sons decapitated
in the marble hall of the Abencirrajas
to ensure the accession of his second wife's child?

Your distaste for oil and perfume, hours spent washing.
My tongue hesitates on the delicate erosion
of your shoulders and lower back.

Even Irving, who rode through bandit country from Seville
and shared the stairs with the Cockle Queen
and her five husbands, knew it had to be iron oxide.

Islands

This passion for iron,
their *metal from heaven,*
the heaviest element
created by fusion
at the heart of a star
which then collapses,
folding and folding

till the core explodes
to scatter and settle
within the triangle
of past, present, future
– all possible worlds.
You dream of islands.
I give you a map
of the Pacific Ocean.
Go there. Come back.

High Water Lines

by Ian McMillan

Lavinia Greenlaw,
Night Photograph,
Faber, £5.99,
ISBN 0 571 16894 9

One of my children said to me the other day, 'I thought you were supposed to be working, You're staring into space'. I ignored her and stared into space, because I was working. Hard. I was reading Lavinia Greenlaw's new book and after each poem I had to just sit and let the poem soak in, like gravy into bread. First poems in books are really important, like first tracks on CD's; they're the *Hello – How are you – This is what I can do.* Greenlaw's first poem, 'Monk on a Tractor', contains at least two of her emblems: water, and statement-as-poetic-line. The poem is about Caldy Island off South Wales, and the monks who live there: 'From April to September, they are surrounded./ The pleasure boat brings holidaymakers,/ who tidy their faces as they go through the gate ...' The poem's vision of the island gets gradually odder – 'The wrong wind brings the wrong things home' – until the last stanza:

Once, a stag swam round the headland.
No one knows where it came from
or who it was that saw it.

It takes a special kind of achieved confidence to allow your poem to walk unaided on such tight, bald lines. I'll just stare into space for a minute.

Many of Greenlaw's poems look at the odd view, and refuse to arrive there by the scenic route: 'Eight months' dust and no electrics./ I rehydrate the lizard in the sink,/ angle it into a sieve and out of sight' ('Spaghetti Western'). Another of her skills is to pile on detail, at its best in the marvellous 'River History', a biography of the Thames full of Greenlawesque statement – 'The Luftwaffe bombed Surrey Commercial Docks/ for fifty-seven nights and the timber blazed / for more days than most people kept counting' – and achieving in the end a kind of euphony in plain wrappers. Hard to imagine, but it works.

One of the many advantages that slim volumes of poetry have over real life is that you can stop and savour a slim volume: 'You're being sent up in Sputnik 2,/ a kind of octopus with rigor mortis' ('For the First Dog in Space'); 'Sea and sky meet in suspension,/ gradual familiar textures of black:/ eel-skin, marble, smoke, oil' ('Night Photograph').

Once you've taken your time with the book, stopped and savoured, stared into space, the poems begin to form part of a whole rather than standing on their own, and the link, I think, is water. Water as redeemer – 'Your touch surprises me/ like a breath of sea air in the city'; as emblem-of-life – 'Beyond the boat, the only interruption/ is the choppy grey-white we leave behind us,/ gone almost before it is gone from sight'; as basis-for-image – 'Out there his boat/ rolls through peaks like a tongue through butter'.

After my children had told me off for staring, one of them caught me standing in the kitchen, reading the book. I showed it to her. She was scornful: 'It's only got 54 pages', she sneered, 'and my school reading book's got 128!' Well, that's true, but these are the weightiest and most satisfying 54 pages I've read in a long time, and I can recommend this book as a book you can swim around, walk slowly through and take your time with. As John Peel once said about an album by Napalm Death, experiencing this is like renting a cottage by the sea.

Bearing True Witness

*Lavinia Greenlaw, in an edited version of her POETS ON POETS talk at the Pegasus Theatre, Oxford, on February 3rd, admires the eloquence and integrity of **Anna Akhmatova***

I doubt Anna Akhmatova had a telephone voice, or particularly good manners, although doubtless she had great dignity. Her poems begin abruptly, without preamble or introduction – the scene is set by the scene itself. Akhmatova's opening lines, through passion, absence or photographic stillness, take us to the heart of a quarrel, to the middle of a forest, to the front line of a war. *Voronezh*, written for the exiled Osip Mandelstam in 1936, begins: 'The whole town stands covered in ice./The trees, the walls, the snow are as though under glass./Tentatively I walk over the crystals' (trans. Peter Norman). These simple phrases are so accurately and carefully chosen that we feel every aspect of the climate: not just the weather but the political temperature, too. Life has literally 'frozen'. Each step is tentative and hazardous.

Akhmatova insisted on clarity, even at the expense of lyrical ease. She had an architectural sense of structure, and a clear eye that was turned on herself as much as on the rest of the world. Her own life, her own location, was the conduit through which she often addressed her subject, be it the loss of a lover, or the enormity of revolution and war. This led to accusations of self-absorption and a concentration on trivia in times of world crisis. In fact her sense of self was a sense of her place in the world, and while often found at the centre of her poems, she is rarely found there alone.

When I was twelve or thirteen, I came across an anthology of modern Russian poetry. In this book of almost a thousand pages, it was the Acmeists that had a lasting impact – their intent on the true nature of things, the value placed on clarity and craft. Mandelstam expressed Acmeism thus: 'No, not the moon, but the dial of a street clock,/ Shines for me'. Akhmatova put it more bluntly: 'only blood smells of blood'. I needed such insistence to give me the courage to move away from imitating poetry to writing my own, but also such constraints to save me from the lowlife romanticism that later replaced my wide-eyed sentimentality. I began to see that Akhmatova could efface her ego enough to look outwards even from the most intimate moments. Seamus Heaney has written of 'the poet's need to get beyond ego in order to become the voice of more than autobiography'. For me part of this means learning to handle reality and the imagination with equal suspicion, and not to be seduced by nostalgia or what I might hope to see in the mirror.

Akhmatova's first collection, *Evening*, was published in 1912 when she was just 23. It was followed by *Rosary*, a wild popular success that also established her unfortunate reputation as a writer of 'women's' subjects: moon, sea and, overwhelmingly, heartbreak. When I discovered her work, I was already feeling uncomfortable about the agenda assigned to women poets and yet here was someone working with all its main themes, whose work I could not put down. Akhmatova rightly loathed being called a 'poetess' and yet her poetry is very much about what is traditionally perceived as a woman's experience and response: 'We don't know how to say goodbye:/we wander on, shoulder to shoulder./Already the sun is going down;/you're moody, I am your shadow' (trans. Stanley Kunitz and Max Hayward). Characteristically, the true dynamics of this poem are hard to grasp, just as Akhmatova herself slipped through the fingers of those critics and fellow writers who would push her into one of the many female stereotypes, who in desperation described her as half nun, half whore. In a 1921 lecture comparing Mayakovsky and Akhmatova, Korney Chukovsky famously compared her to a nun who crosses herself while kissing her lover. To his regret, this contradictory image was subsequently used in the post-revolutionary world of manifestoes, to condemn her for a lack of clarity and commitment, for an inability to declare a stance and stick to it at all artistic costs. Stalin, Trotsky and the new Soviet critique had no time for such an insistently individual voice.

Despite this, it has come to be recognized that her later work, in particular *Requiem* and *Poem Without a Hero* stand as some of the finest testaments to the unimaginable upheaval that her generation endured. And the power of such work does indeed appear to come not only from her belief in her fated purpose to witness and give expression to such events, but also from the way in which these vast subjects are anchored in her self.

The revolution and war that abruptly ended Akhmatova's carefree and cosmopolitan early life were followed by the execution of her first husband, the poet Nikolay Gumilev, World War II, the repeated imprisonment of her son, poverty, hunger, homelessness, and the constant fear and helplessness of waiting out the Terror. Her work was tacitly banned and publicly condemned. For fifteen years she was unable to publish and it is astonishing to find that in spite of all this, and the persecution that many poets faced at that time, she continued to write.

Akhmatova's pursuit of her vocation against all odds and in the face of considerable risk throws into stark relief the choices any writer has to make. For contemporary British poets the implications of these are comparatively trivial yet there is much to learn from a poet who wrote directly about her craft, and of its demands upon her, amplified as they were by historical circumstance: the insistence on freedom and solitude, the crippling but somehow essential piece of ice in the heart, and the need despite all this to live a real life, to be close to family, friends, lovers and children. Akhmatova paid more than most for her vocation: 'If you can't give me love and peace/ Then give me bitter fame'.

I recently heard the African commentator Ronald Segal use Akhmatova as a model of the role of the writer in revolutionary times. He quoted Trotsky's scornful dismissal of her work and went on to speak of her human impact, her commitment to the truth of the writer who like her should do no more and no less than 'use words for what they are meant to mean'. My affection for the young Akhmatova grew to admiration when I read her later work and found that here was a poet who could take on such historical and misused themes, and events of such enormity, and transmute them through the absolute ordinary truth of what it means to live through war and revolution, from abstracts into living moments. Why deal with abstracts when there is nothing to burn and nothing to eat?

Requiem is full of such painful directness and yet there is no self-pity, just a philosophical sense that all experience must mean something, though quite what is never easy to answer. Imperious visionary, icon to some, this sequence also shows something of the Akhmatova that Lidiya Chukovskaya describes in her journals: anxious, vulnerable, scared of crossing the street alone or falling downstairs in the dark.

For Akhmatova and her contemporaries language was literally dangerous. Poems were secretly composed, furtively scribbled, memorized by the poet and their friends, and the pages hurriedly destroyed. Poems had to be memorable, as they had to be remembered. A subversive or cynical allusion, however obscure, could result in arrest, exile or death not only for the writer but also for their family.

And yet I do not speak her language. I studied Russian at school for two years and sadly only remember enough to get a rough notion of what the original text sounds like. At least this gives me some idea of rhythm, meter and rhyme. Each translator has to make choices about how they balance form with meaning, impulse with sense. All are attuned to the poetic ear of their country, culture and generation. I have my favourites – those I knew first and those who speak to me most eloquently. And having read across these different versions, I have gone from being shaken by the realization of how broad an interpretation can be, to being assured of a fundamental and immutable voice that is present in different ways in all of them. Akhmatova, like Pasternak, used formal rhyme far more than most English translations convey. But formal rhyme seems less trite or strained in the Russian language, where constantly changing word-endings give the poet a greater freedom and access to more natural harmonics.

Conventional poetic subjects are the most difficult to approach. Readers come to such work with a map of tradition in their hands and may follow their own signposts, missing yours completely. Poets return to worn out themes with the need to convey them in a new way. This too often takes the form of satire, bathos and witty inversion. It is harder to do it straight. Akhmatova, ironically seen by many of her contemporaries as the keeper of the classical flame while Mayakovsky (privately a great admirer of her work) ran around letting off Futurist fireworks, was a true innovator who renewed many traditional themes with ease. Her work is so immediate, full of such accuracy and intent, that she had no need for novelty. There was no need to dazzle her readers when her writing was full of such natural wonder.

Akhmatova's work culminated in the long sequence *Poem without a hero*, on which she worked from 1940 to 1962, in Leningrad, Tashkent (the eastern city to which she was evacuated) and Moscow. It is dedicated to her friends and fellow citizens who perished in Leningrad during the siege. It is in this complex and difficult work, packed with erudite allusion, encompassing a range of voices, personae and form, that Akhmatova moves towards a resolution of both her central themes and the various aspects of her craft. She allows herself unusual freedom. She has earnt it:

> The poem does not have any third, seventh, or
>   twenty-ninth meanings.
> I shall neither change it nor explain it
> What I have written – I have written.

W. N. HERBERT
Forked Tongue

W.N. HERBERT WAS BORN IN DUNDEE IN 1961 AND WENT TO OXFORD IN 1979. HE WAS CHOSEN for *Poetry Review*'s 'New Poets '92' issue in Autumn 1992. His poetry includes: *Sharawaggi* (with Robert Crawford, Polygon, 1990), *Dundee Doldrums* (Galliard, 1991) *Anither Music* (Venell Press, 1991) and two new collections – *The Testament of Reverend Thomas Dick* (Arc) and *Forked Tongue* (Bloodaxe); the latter is reviewed by Edwin Morgan on page 110.

W.N. Herbert is essentially an avant-garde poet with populist tendencies. His early poetry is entirely in Scots – not the street-talk of the Scottish layman but an uncommon parlance construed chiefly from scholarly reference books; the resultant argot is then 'translated' back into the market-place, there to quarrel with its peers. Herbert is an eloquent advocate of Scottish Scots (as opposed to the mere dialect of Scottish English) and an admirer of MacDiarmid and the American L=A=N=G=U=A=G=E poets. Poems such as 'Mappamundi', 'Hawthornden Morning Blues' and 'Ode to Tesco's' can be read phonetically but many of his Scots poems are more densely allusive; his statement that 'These Doldrums ur frae ivry toun in Scoatlan –/Inglann tae, or onywhere' is a mite disingenuous in the circumstances. The notion of linguistic authenticity is something of a red herring in Herbert's case; it is the very artificiality of The Word which he revels in, replacing a stereotypical Calvinist work-aesthetic with an idiosyncratic play-aesthetic of his own. His poetry is, in Wallace Stevens' precise sense, a 'fictive music' and in general prefers elegant apocrypha to ugly gospels. As he writes in 'A Portrait Skull, New Guinea': 'I recognize the need in me/to scratch back beauty from the dirt,/not for the truth at all but for/desire itself, the oldest narrator'. Herbert's intellectual zest and sense of fun is omnipresent – 'The Cortina Sonata' (his English sequence in *Forked Tongue*) ranges from Fra Angelica to Eric Morecambe – but his greatest asset is his ability to *surprise*, either with an inexplicable juxtaposition or a shot of unexpected simplicity: 'A woman chalks hopscotch on/the Campo for a child, then hops'. **(KJ)**

W.N. Herbert writes:
Picture this: the Picts were not absorbed into the general population of Scotland, but remained tribal, Jewish, and ran the chip shops. Their enigmatic symbols now mean 'Frying Tonite'. The Scots did not abandon their language, and in any pub in Dundee men say 'Aye, Eh wiz at thi dirrye dantoun yestreen richt eneuch'. And are not beaten up. John Knox had a horse's tail sprouting from his coccyx which he kept trimmed short like a hoover attachment. Aliens from the planet Zog landed last Wednesday and implanted the concept of capitalism in everyone's brains. Just before *Star Trek* last week we were living in a moneyless stateless society. Oh, and Mozart's father was a tree surgeon; Captain Beefheart went to my school; Iggy

Pop is in telepathic contact with the bottlenose dolphins in the Moray Firth. And Mark E. Smith is the editor of *Poetry Review*.

This is the world which I attempt to create by writing in both Scots and English. This is the world you will help nudge into existence if you read my books. The decision ... is your's.

Three influential 20th C. books:
Complete Poems of Hugh MacDiarmid, *Complete Poems* of Edwin Morgan, *Collected Poems* of Frank O'Hara. (Contained in microdots strategically positioned in each book would be the complete works of Rilke, Mayakovsky, and Liz Lochhead.)

THREE POEMS BY W. N. HERBERT

The King and Queen of Dumfriesshire

The King and Queen of Dumfriesshire sit
in their battery-dead Triumph, gazing ahead
at an iced-over windscreen like a gull rolled flat.
They are cast in bronze, with Henry Moore holes
shot in each other by incessant argument;
these are convenient for holding her tartan flask,
his rolled-up *Scotsman*. The hairy skeleton
of a Border terrier sits in the back window,
not nodding. On the back seat rests
their favourite argument, the one about
how he does not permit her to see the old friends
she no longer likes and he secretly misses;
the one which is really about punishing each other
for no longer wanting to make love.
The argument is in the form of a big white bowl
with a black band around it hand-painted with fruit.
It has a gold rim, and in it lies
a brown curl of water from the leaking roof.
Outside, the clouds continue
to bomb the glen with sheep, which bare
their slate teeth as they tumble,
unexpectedly sneering.
The King and Queen of Dumfriesshire sit
like the too-solid bullet-ridden ghosts
of Bonny and Clyde, not eating their
tinned salmon sandwiches, crustless, still
wrapped in tinfoil, still in the tupperware.
They survey their domain, not glancing at
each other, not removing from the glove compartment
any of the old words they have always used
to keep their only threat at bay: of separation.

Riddle to my Wife in Brazil

Why is ut that we anely seem tae meet
at a narra hoose wi nae windies
an twa wee doors at either end?

Mony fowk cam oot thi wan door
Eh nivir saw gang in,
but nane o them hae ony fisses:

mebbe thae daurk waas ur hingin wi
thir cast-aff glances,
yir ain dear glisk amang them.

Eh treh tae gang in thi ithir wey,
but Eh jist arrehv baneliss
ootben anither fremit hoose.

Let's no meet lyk this ony mair:
come ti me smilin thru wir bedroom door.

(Glisk—look, expression; fremit—foreign, strange.)

Poem to my Wife in China

Whit's thi difference
atween
thi ambir glaze
oan ma favourite tea bowl
i thi Ashmolean
and
thi drucken sheen
oan Li Po's een
as he fell
intil thi mune-filled river?

Thi answer is
Eh dinna ken
thi colour o
thi poet's eyes
but Eh do know hoo
ut feels
tae ettle tae catch
yir luvir's fiss
i thi depths
o a whisky gless.

(Atween—between; drucken—drunken; een—eyes; ettle—attempt.)

Lingua Scozzese
by Edwin Morgan

W. N. Herbert
Forked Tongue,
Bloodaxe, £7.95,
ISBN 1 85224 267 1

This is a substantial collection from the sprightly author of *Dundee Doldrums* and *Anither Music* (both 1991). The title refers to the fact that half of the book is in English and half in Scots, and the furcatory approach is both exposition and exploration of a linguistic identity that cannot but be unsettled but can make its clash of crack a struck spark. Herbert's positive attitude to bilingualism is taken further in 'Other tongues', where a search is acknowledged, through a Demosthenean dialogue with a pebble, for something beyond authenticity: 'I have another tongue in my head/the like of which it's never heard'. The English poems, set partly in the poet's home town of Dundee and partly in Venice and Corfu, have a strong sense of the atmosphere of place (with just very occasionally a traveloguish touch – 'Joyce taught English there'), but more particularly a sense of time and memory, of the generations, of children and grandparents and aunts and uncles, of the speaker's father driving into the back of a pig in Ireland, of a waiter flicking a wasp (and more) out of his mother's bikini top, of the boy waiting his turn on a painted metal rocking-horse.

A measured pathos is highly effective in reminiscences of characters, like Isabella who

> reassured us
> with peppery soup, kail and lentils,
> that nourishment could never end.
> And yet leukemia ate through you
>
> into our safe lustrum; in all the photos
> you are whiter than our smiles.
> The ward was built on artificial slopes;
> we rolled down them as you died.
> ('The Beano elegies')

As we draw near the end of the first (English) part of the book, warnings and annunciations of the second part begin to appear. 'Other tongues', quoted above, allows the loquacious and sardonic Greek pebble to nag the poet, a wandering Scot, telling him that 'other tongues gall you because / you've spent so much time / shuffling the beach of your own'. And the excellent 'Dingle Dell', set in Brechin, dismisses both the half-understood historical reality of a tenth-century round tower and the couthy stereotypes of peasant figures on a nineteenth-century clock in favour of 'something / between troughs, a green word dancing', a Dingle Dell, a Bella as the name shared by both his grandmothers, a place that reveals itself through what people say: 'There is no passport to this country,/it exists as a quality of the language'. Perhaps there should be a passport! But in the meantime, there is language: Scottish English; various kinds of Scots; Gaelic. Herbert is one of a number of young Scottish writers who welcome the diversity and refuse to be browbeaten by the either/ or tauromachies of earlier decades. His use of Scots takes every kind of risk, and the expected taunt of dictionary-dredging is met head on by a vivid Scots version of Pablo Neruda's 'Ode to the Dictionary', where *tu antigua madera* becomes 'yir birkenshaw o Caledon', and *fecundas en la fronda del lenguaje* is 'a goshens o speak i thi blauds'. Glossaries are provided, but with some of the more densely textured poems, both goodwill and hard work are demanded. However, even an initially scowling reader will soon be wooed by the energetic rhythms, the striking sound-effects, the sense of imaginative daring which seems to be released through defamiliarization. Perseverance with 'The landfish', the longest and most impressive of these poems, reveals a wild, bizarre yet moving narrative of the old whaling days (once very important to Scotland), enriched with hints of Jonah, Melville, and the Ancient Mariner. The Dundonian voice (e.g. 'Eh' for 'I', 'meh' for 'my') is never lost, and a local underpinning is strengthened by the embedding within the poem of passages taken from *The Complaynt of Scotland* (c.1550), a verbally cascading prose work written probably by a fellow-Dundonian, Robert Wedderburn.

As in so many Scottish poets, the energy also works through comedy. 'Hawthornden Morning Blues' laments how the amenities of this writer's retreat fail to unjam writer's block:

> Oh Lord therr is a spidir
> and she's drinkan frae ma hert;
> Oh Lord therr is a spidir
> sookan bluid oot o ma hert;
> gin you cud skelp that spidir
> that wid shairly be a stert.

This is a vigorous and challenging volume; highly recommended.

CAROL ANN DUFFY
Mean Time

CAROL ANN DUFFY WAS BORN IN GLASGOW IN 1955. SHE MOVED TO STAFFORDSHIRE AS A CHILD AND read Philosophy at Liverpool University. In 1983 she won first prize in the National Poetry Competition and has since won very many prizes, including the Whitbread Award and the Forward Prize for *Mean Time* (Anvil, 1993). Her earlier books are *Standing Female Nude* (1985), *Selling Manhattan* (1987), and *The Other Country* (1990), all published by Anvil Press. Her *Selected Poems* is due from Penguin in August.

Carol Ann Duffy burst onto the scene in the early '80s with poems in voices that were brutal and tender by turns: a hard man patronizing his wife ('Dinner on the table and a clean shirt/but I respect her point of view'), a psychopath ('When I zip up the leather, I'm in a new skin'), or a servant wearing her mistress's pearls to keep them warm ('All night/I feel their absence and I burn'). The vigour, directness and psychological insight of these poems stamped her out as a great original. With her four books her range has steadily extended: some of the poems in *The Other Country* and *Mean Time* have an almost Larkinesque nostalgia and pathos. The voices now include, much of the time, her own. She also writes poems for our times of great generality: 'Translating the English, 1989' is a monologue which holds up a hideous distorted mirror to English Society. The voice is that of an atrocious interpreter-cum-tout and what it is saying is too concentrated an essence of sleaze to be true. You want to think. But it is. (She often writes like this In short. Sometimes one word. Sentences.) Monologue has also led her to riddle poems, like 'The Legend', in which the elephant is described as if already extinct. It is one of the few really effective green poems in existence; it does what only a poem can do, make you see afresh: 'But people have always lied. You know some say it had a trunk/like a soft telescope, that it looked up along it at the sky, /and balanced a bright, gone star on the end, and it died'. **(PF)**

Carol Ann Duffy writes:

The poems in *Mean Time* are about the different ways in which time brings about change or loss. In the collection, I mean to write about time. The effects of time can be mean. Mean can mean average. The events in the poems can happen to the average woman or man. The dwindling of childhood. Ageing. The distance of history. The tricks of memory and the renewal of language. The end of love. Divorce. New love. Luck. And so on. In the last book I published with Anvil, *The Other Country*, I had begun to write more personal, auto-

biographical poems; and this switch from the dramatic-monologue dominated stance of earlier collections is intensified in *Mean Time*. I found it interesting that the techniques stumbled across and re-fined in writing 'Other Voices' helped me to pitch my own voices – for we all have several – particularly when finding language for the painful areas dealt with in the poems 'Adultery' and 'Disgrace'.

Lastly, I have tried to order the poems in *Mean Time* in such a way that the collection shares the coherence of a record album; that it reads with some kind of emotional, not literal, narrative. Opening with Manfred Mann's 'Do Wah Diddy Diddy' and closing with the quieter place names of the shipping forecast – familiar from the radio – *Mean Time* tries to record the brief words we hear and speak under the clock. In that effort, at least, I hope it is optimistic.

(Reprinted from the *Poetry Book Society Bulletin*, Summer 1993)

Three influential 20th C. books:
Aimé Cesaire, *Return to my Native Land*; Pablo Neruda, *Twenty Love Poems and a Song of Despair*; W. S. Graham, *Implements in their Places*.

Do you feel a special poetic affinity towards any of your contemporaries?
'I've felt part of a distinct new energy in poetry for the last decade, and this would include black writers going backwards from Zephaniah, Irish writers (Kennelly, Durcan, Boland, Rita Ann Higgins), Welsh poets (Robert Minhinnick, Duncan Bush), poets over 40 too numerous to mention. There are some excellent poets amongst the New Generation but the list itself misses the point. Performance poets like Liz Lochhead, Ian McMillan have improved things for all of us.'

From a list of twelve movements and key anthologies this century, Carol Ann Duffy selected 1920s modernism, Louis MacNeice from the Auden Generation, the Beats, the Liverpool poets, and Bloodaxe's *Sixty Women Poets* for positive mention.

TWO POEMS BY CAROL ANN DUFFY

Mrs Midas

It was late September. I'd just poured a glass of wine, begun
to unwind, while the vegetables cooked. The kitchen
filled with smell of itself, relaxed, its steamy breath
gently blanching the windows. So I opened one,
then with my fingers wiped the other's glass like a brow.
He was standing under the pear tree snapping a twig.

Now the garden was long and the visibility poor, the way
the dark of the ground seems to drink the light of the sky,
but that twig in his hand was gold. And then he plucked
a pear from a branch, we grew Fondante d'Automne,
and it sat in his palm like a lightbulb. On.
I thought to myself Is he putting fairy-lights in the tree?

He came in to the house. The doorknobs gleamed.
He drew the blinds. You know the mind; I thought of
the Field of the Cloth of Gold and of Miss Macready.
He sat in that chair like a king on a burnished throne.
The look on his face was strange, wild, vain; I said
What in the name of God is going on? He started to laugh.

I served up the meal. For starters, corn on the cob.
Within seconds he was spitting out the teeth of the rich.
He toyed with his spoon, then mine, then with the knives, the forks.
He asked where was the wine. I poured with a shaking hand,
a fragrant, bone-dry white from Italy, then watched
as he picked up the glass, goblet, golden chalice, drank.

It was then that I started to scream. He sank to his knees.
After we'd both calmed down, I finished the wine
on my own, hearing him out. I made him sit

on the other side of the room and keep his hands to himself.
I locked the cat in the cellar. I moved the phone.
The toilet I didn't mind. I couldn't believe my ears:

how he'd had a wish. Look, we all have wishes; granted.
But who has wishes granted? Him. Do you know about gold?
It feeds no-one; aurum, soft, untarnishable; slakes
no thirst. He tried to light a cigarette; I gazed, entranced,
as the blue flame played on its luteous stem. At least,
I said, you'll be able to give up smoking for good.

Separate beds. In fact, I put a chair against my door,
near petrified. He was below, turning the spare room
into the tomb of Tutankhamen. You see, we were passionate then,
in those halcyon days; unwrapping each other, rapidly,
like presents, fast food. But now I feared his honeyed embrace,
the kiss that would turn my lips to a work of art.

And who, when it comes to the crunch, can live
with a heart of gold? That night, I dreamt I bore
his child, its perfect ore limbs, its little tongue
like a precious latch, its amber eyes
holding their pupils like flies. My dream-milk
burned in my breasts. I woke to the streaming sun.

So he had to move out. We'd a caravan
in the wilds, in a glade of its own. I drove him up
under cover of dark. He sat in the back.
And then I came home, the woman who married the fool
who wished for gold. At first, I visited, odd times,
parking the car a good way off, then walking.

You knew you were getting close. Golden trout
on the grass. One day, a hare hung from a larch,
a beautiful lemon mistake. And then his footprints,
glistening next to the river's path. He was thin,
delirious; hearing, he said, the music of Pan
from the woods. Listen. That was the last straw.

What gets me now is not the idiocy or greed
but lack of thought for me. Pure selfishness. I sold
the contents of the house and came down here.
I think of him in certain lights, dawn, late afternoon,
and once a bowl of apples stopped me dead. I miss most,
even now, his hands, his warm hands on my skin, his touch.

(This poem was first published in the *TLS*.)

Away and See

Away and see an ocean suck at a boiled sun
and say to someone things I'd blush even to dream.
Slip off your dress in a high room over the harbour.
Write to me soon.

New fruits sing on the flipside of night in a market
of language, light, a tune from the chapel nearby
stopping you dead, the peach in your palm respiring.
Taste it for me.

Away and see the things that words give a name to, the flight
of syllables, wingspan stretching a noun. Test words
wherever they live; listen and touch, smell, believe.
Spell them with love.

Skedaddle. Somebody chaps at the door at a year's end,
     hopeful.
Away and see who it is. Let in the new, the vivid,
horror and pity, passion, the stranger holding the future.
Ask him his name.

Nothing's the same as anything else. Away and see
for yourself. Walk. Fly. Take a boat till land reappears,
altered forever, ringing its bells, alive. Go on. G'on. Gon.
Away and see.

(Reprinted by permission of Anvil Press from *Mean Time*.)

NAMING OF POETS

Although some names make it regardless of a common-or-garden ring (Snodgrass springs to mind instantly) you'll probably stand a better chance if you were born with or acquire a more exotic one. Attila sounds immediately noticeable, as does Jean Binta Breeze, whereas names such as John Major or John Smith would be unlikely to be recognized because unmemorable – in Britain at least.

It's good to be born with a name like Eva Salzman or Moniza Alvi - but note that when Moniza is misprinted as Monica it loses some of its appeal. However, many good names are acquired by marriage and retained beyond. Satyamurti, Kazantzis, Jackowska can serve as examples to us all. Also Byron (Catherine) has that certain inexplicable 'something'. Sometimes you need only change your first name though. A poet of my acquaintance got her name in print the minute she adopted 'Berenice' instead of 'Beryl'. Just the French touch – as in Michèle (Roberts) – can be helpful. Anything unEnglish or zanily English (eg, 'Stockbroker') can serve you well. Scottish, Irish and Welsh names always welcome of course. There's no way of accounting for the perennial appeal of contemporary names like Adcock, Stevenson, Duffy, Reading, Smith (Ken), Cope, Bartlett, Fanthorpe, Brown (Jacqueline). I could go on and on ... It doesn't make sense, but it is not the business of this article – or even, incidentally, of poetry – to make sense.

If you attend readings, you will have noticed that the most durable names are the ones in sturdy footwear – very necessary for humping books around in order to perform one's name in public. Once you've made it as a jobbing/jogging name it doesn't matter much how you look, though, and age doesn't count. (This has to be said quickly before readers rudely start calculating the real age of some of the NEW GEN 'all under 40' names.) You don't necessarily have to be a good poet, of course. One of the worst mere *poems* I've glanced at is by someone called Elizabeth Regina I. This proves my point. It's that foreign name, 'Regina', that counts – and who cares how old she is?

Sylvia Kantaris

CALENDAR OF EVENTS
may

1st BRISTOL
Simon Armitage, Michael Donaghy, Lavinia Greenlaw, Kathleen Jamie. BBC Bristol, Whiteladies Road, Bristol. *7.30pm. Admission free. Tel. 0272 742134.*

3rd LONDON
Elizabeth Garrett, Mick Imlah, Don Paterson, Pauline Stainer. The Chelsfield Room, South Bank Centre, London SE1. *7.30pm. £5/£3.50 concessions. Tel 071 928 8800.*

NEWCASTLE
Lavinia Greenlaw, W.N. Herbert, Sarah Maguire. The Bridge Hotel, Castle Square, Newcastle. *8.00pm. £4.50/£3.50. Tel. 091 232 5988*

MANCHESTER
John Burnside, Ian Duhig, Michael Hofmann, Jamie McKendrick. Waterstone's Booksellers, 91 Deansgate, Manchester. *7.00pm. £2. Tel. 061 832 1992.*

GLASGOW
Robert Crawford, Michael Donaghy, Kathleen Jamie. Moir Hall, Granville Street, Glasgow. *7.30pm. £4/£2. Tel. 041 227 5033.*

OXFORD
Moniza Alvi, Simon Armitage, David Dabydeen, Glyn Maxwell. Blackwell's Bookshop, 50 Broad Street, Oxford. *7.00pm. £1. Tel. 0865 792792.*

5th LEEDS
Simon Armitage, Elizabeth Garrett, Pauline Stainer.
Waterstone's Booksellers, 36/38 Albion Street, Leeds. *7.00pm. £1. Tel. 0532 420 839*

6th HULL
Michael Donaghy, Kathleen Jamie, Sarah Maguire. The Mortimer Suite, City Hall. *8.00pm. Tel. 0482 226655. (Organized by Bête Noire).*

9th BIRMINGHAM
John Burnside, Glyn Maxwell, Sarah Maguire. Birmingham Readers and Writers Festival, Midland Arts Gentre, Cannon Hill Park, Birmingham, *9.00 pm. £4.50/£2.75. Tel. 021 235 4244*

ABERDEEN
Mick Imlah, Don Paterson. Poems & Pints, Ma Cameron's Inn, Little Belmont Street, Aberdeen. *7.30pm. Admission free. Tel. 0224 634622 (Organised by Aberdeen Central Library.*

10th BRIGHTON
Simon Armitage, David Dabydeen, Lavinia Greenlaw. Preceded by discussion, chaired by Melvyn Bragg, with judges James Wood and Vicki Feaver. Brighton Festival, The Richmond, Richmond Place, Brighton. *7.30 pm £5/£4 Tel 0273 709709.*

SWINDON
Sarah Maguire. Link Studio, West Swindon. *7.30pm £3. Tel. 0793 871111.*

OXFORD
Elizabeth Garret, Jamie McKendrick, Mick Imlah. Freud's Cafe, Walton Street. *Admission free, 7.00pm. Tel. 0865 792792.*

11th BIRMINGHAM
Simon Armitage. In discussion with Sue Roberts, Roland Keating, Chris Meade and Peter Symes. Birmingham Readers and Writers Festival, Midland Arts Centre, Cannon Hill Park, Birmingham. *7.30pm. £3.75/£2.50. Tel. 021 235 4244*

12th LEEDS
Lavinia Greenlaw, Michael Hofmann, Glyn Maxwell.
Waterstone's Booksellers, 36/38 Albion Street, Leeds. *7.00pm. £1. Tel. 0532 420839.*

READING
Elizabeth Garrett. Rising Sun Institute, 30 Silver Street, Reading. *8pm. £2.50/£2. Tel. 0734 866788*

14th MIDDLESBOROUGH
Moniza Alvi, Glyn Maxwell, Robert Crawford. Small Presses Festival, Middlesborough Town Hall, Corporation Street, Middlesbrough, *8pm £4/£2. Tel. 0642 812288.*

15th LONDON
Carol Ann Duffy, Michael Donaghy. Greenwich Theatre, Crooms Hill, SE10. *6.30pm. £5/£3. 081 858 7755.*

16th ABERDEEN
Robert Crawford, Kathleen Jamie, W.N. Herbert. Aberdeen Central Library, Rosemount Viaduct, Aberdeen. *7.00pm. Admission free. Tel. 0224 634622.*

17th LONDON
Simon Armitage, Glyn Maxwell, Don Paterson. Waterstone's Booksellers, 121 Charing Cross Road, WC2. *7.30 pm. £2. Tel. 071 434 4291.*

18th LONDON
John Burnside, Don Paterson, Lavinia Greenlaw. Waterstone's Booksellers, 128 Camden High Street NW1. *7pm. £2. Tel. 071 284 4948.*

DUNDEE
W. N. Herbert. Waterstone's Booksellers, 35 Commercial Street, Dundee. *7.00pm. £2. Tel. 0382 200322.*

19th YORK
Simon Armitage, Ian Duhig. Waterstone's Booksellers, 28-29 High Ousegate, York. *7.00pm. £2. Tel. 0904 628740.*

EXETER
Don Paterson, Michael Donaghy. Cabaret Theatre, Exeter & Devon Arts Centre, Gandy Street *8.00pm. £4/£3. 0392 421111.*

20th REDDITCH
Michael Donaghy, Sarah Maguire, Jamie McKendrick. Redditch Library, Market Place. *7pm. £3/£1.50. Tel. 0527 63291.*

22nd HAY-ON-WYE
Michael Donaghy, Michael Hofmann, Kathleen Jamie. The Hay Festival, Midland Marquee, Hay-on-Wye. *12 noon. £4. 0497 821 299.*

24th DUNDEE
Robert Crawford, W. N. Herbert, Kathleen Jamie, Don Paterson. Waterstone's Booksellers, 35 Commercial Street, Dundee. *7.00pm. Admission free. Tel. 0382 200322.*

25th TUNBRIDGE WELLS
Susan Wicks, Hammick's Bookshop, 119 Mount Pleasant Rd, Tunbridge Wells, Kent, *6.30pm. Admission free. Tel. 0892 536707.*

26th FIRLE, nr LEWES
Carol Ann Duffy (with Jackie Kay, Vicki Feaver). Charleston Festival, Charleston Farmhouse, Firle, nr. Lewes. *7.30pm. £4.95. Tel. 0273 709709 .*

SALISBURY
Mick Imlah, Susan Wicks, Glyn Maxwell. Salberg Studio, Salisbury Playhouse, Malthouse Lane. *7.45pm. Tel. 0722 320333.*

27th DORCHESTER
Glyn Maxwell. Dorchester Arts Centre, School Lane, The Grove. *7.30pm. £3. Tel. 0305 266926.*

These details are correct at the time of going to press. Further events may be added. For information, ring the New Generation Events Hotline: 071 240 2133.

NATIONAL POETRY COMPETITION

The 1993 National Poetry Competition, supported by the Guardian, was memorable for producing a very fine winning poem by an unknown poet. Sam Gardiner was born in Northern Ireland in 1936. He has lived and worked as an architect in London and Lincolnshire. He has recently begun to write and two poems have appeared in the Spectator. 'Protestant Windows', which won the £3000 First Prize, was given a memorable reading by Sean O'Brien at the prize-giving on January 17th, presided over by Miroslav Holub. Second Prize (£500) went to Eva Salzman, no stranger to these pages, for 'Alex, Tiffany, Meg', and third, to Kathleen Jamie, one of the New Generation Poets. Kathleen's poem 'Mr and Mrs Scotland are Dead' appears with her other poems on page 14. We print here the First and Second Prize winners.

The judges were Sean O'Brien, Helen Dunmore and Anthony Thwaite. The other prize winners were: (£100) Simon Anten, Don Burbidge, C. L. Dallat, Michael Donaghy (for 'Caliban's Books', see page 63), John Gurney, John Haynes, David Kennedy, James Lasdun, Andrew Stibbs, and Emily Taylor. Commended were: Sue Cooper, Matthew Francis, Patricia McCarthy, Eddie McMoon, Don Paterson (for '11:0 Baldovan', see page 21), Matthew Sweeney, Michael Symmons Roberts, Robin Robertson, Padraig Rooney, and Eric Smith.

Protestant Windows, The Competition Anthology, includes all the prize winners, and is available, price £4.25, from: The National Poetry Competition, The Poetry Society, 22 Betterton Street, London WC2H 9BU.

SAM GARDINER
Protestant Windows

They come at sunset peddling daylight, two
Salesmen wearing glasses, through which they view
His shabby sliding sashes with disdain.
'Wood?' they suppose and feign
Dismay. 'Yes, comes from trees',
And he raises the drawbridge ten degrees,
A hurdle to reservists
But child's play to front line evangelists
With news of paradise
On earth (at this address to be precise)
In whitest white PVC.
                            'Think of all
The blessings. And if economical
Heavenly comfort isn't what you need
Think of Our Earth', they plead,
And their plastic-rimmed, double, glazed eyes glow
With love for generations of window
Salesmen as yet unborn. 'If I were you,
I'd save my CO_2
For atheists and papists. I doubt
They even know about
King Billy'. 'Who?' 'William III to you
Brought sliding sashes to

Britain, fetched in pure air and sanity.
Without him we'd still be
In the dark.'
'Sorry, we must go. It's late',
They say, and beat a retreat to the gate,
And pause. Quick as a flash
He raises an effortlessly sliding sash
For a parting shot. 'Plastic heretics!'
He shouts. The window sticks.
He tugs, a sash-cord snaps, the window drops
On his head, where it stops.
Latimer and Ridley know how he feels
As bloodied, martyred for his faith, he reels
Towards eternity,
Where planets, the latest novelty,
Are looking less and less
Like being a success.

EVA SALZMAN
Alex, Tiffany, Meg

rode fast convertibles, rose up like the Furies
blazing scarves and halters in a fire-trail.
The local boys, at first no more than curious,
went mad for the sting in their beautiful tails.

Such kindly girls; they deftly wound my hair
with strange accessories. Naked, like stone,
I bore the slender fingers and thundery stares
as they ripped and ripped away at my bikini-line.

Not ugly, nor evil, they were taken so seriously
their shadows slip beneath each lover, the fates
re-grouping nightly, featured in the crumpled sheets
or the legacy of silk, my abandoned freight.
Pursued or in pursuit, I find your street
and fly into your bed. Calm this fury, please.

Entry Forms for the 1994 National Poetry Competition are now available. The Competition will be run in association with BBC Radio 4. *Stanza's* **producer, Sue Roberts, will chair the judging panel: Fleur Adcock, Lemn Sissay, and Jackie Kay. The first poem submitted costs £4.00, subsequent poems £3.00. Poetry Society members are allowed a** *second poem* **free. This offer also applies to members who join the Poetry Society at the time of submitting poems to the Competition. For an entry form send an SAE to: The National Poetry Competition, 22 Betterton Street, London WC2H 9BU, or ring the Poetry Society Hotline – 071 240 2133 – and leave a message.**

JOHN HEGLEY
Birthday in a Roman Garden

At their meeting
she gives him a greeting
and a broach wrapped in a colourful
papyrus.
It is easily opened;
it has not been sealed with Sellotape.
He attaches the gift to his garment,
lifts his head
and feels the sea of inner sickness
as he sees on her person
the small red flower of another person's
passion.
'Where did you get it?' he blurts
and he hurts.
'The market in Ostia', she replies.
'I mean the love-bite not the present,
whose is it?'
'It is mine,' she answers.
And for her intelligence he is thankful
and for her infidelity he is not.
He returns the broach
and turns in his toga towards the sun
ignoring all of her imploring him to stay,
of which there is none.

Verse is a Cabaret ...
Sue Hubbard goes to a John Hegley gig

INSIDE EVERY FUNNY MAN, IT SEEMS, THERE IS A serious man clamouring to get out. Not content with being one of cinema's greatest comic writers Woody Allen has immortal longings to be Bergman and Jonathan Miller eschewed student reviews and 'Beyond the Fringe' for opera and pontification. Inside the quirky persona of John Hegley, there is a poet demanding acknowledgement. What is this desire for gravitas? Isn't it enough, in this sad world, to make people laugh?

For John Hegley is very funny indeed. Not when you meet him, not when he is just John Hegley on a Thursday morning having a cup of coffee in a North London café talking about humour and looking as if he has just dragged himself out of bed. Then he is rather nervous, almost tense, but when he is John Hegley the performer. From the moment he came on stage at the Bloomsbury Theatre in his recent show 'Winter Warmer' he captured the audience. 'They have a dog ...' he announced completely deadpan. Not an intrinsically witty line perhaps, but there were immediate guffaws of laughter. Standing in his slightly wimpish, buttoned-up suit, a skinny figure with tousled hair and in *those* glasses, Hegley knows the comic value of the little man, the underdog, the runt against the world. Despite coming from the New Comedy stable, he continues a particularly English line of lovable victims, that has spawned comics such as Norman Wisdom and Tony Hancock.

Hegley elevates the ordinary, the 'lower-middle class', the suburban to create a cult of the banal. Glasses, garden sheds, primary school – his humour flourishes in a prepubescent world of pets and teachers, where emotion is best expressed by kicking the girl you fancy on the shins under your school desk.

There exists a boundary beyond which he warns his audience not to trespass: 'Talking about my feelings ain't my cup of tea' ... 'because revealing how I'm feeling it isn't my Darjeeling'. Yet behind this disclaimer one senses the pain, the poignancy of a certain childhood isolation. The jokes about school and glasses ('The first time I walked on stage/ someone called out "hey/ look it's Buddy Holly!"' / It's not what you'd expect in a nativity play') emphasize this and are funnier because we are invited, up to a point, to share this vulnerability. Over our coffee he quotes Elvis Costello who felt he was invisible until he took up rock 'n roll when he was eighteen.

Hegley is a master of bathos, anti-climax. He shares this – and his playful, apparently guileless rhythms – with that most unlikely of literary bed-fellows, Stevie Smith. Take Smith's 'The Bereaved Swan': 'Wan/Swan/On the lake/Like a cake/Of soap/Why is the swan/Wan/On the lake?/He has abandoned hope', or 'The wood was rather old and dark/The witch was very ugly/And if it hadn't been for father/Walking there so smugly/I never should have followed/The beckoning of her finger' ('The Little Boy Lost'). One can sense the same device being used in Hegley's 'Summer': 'the fan heater gathers dust/the dusk/gathers later/than in winter/and the elastic gathers my underpants/much the same all year round'.

John Hegley has an obvious love/hate relationship with poetry. He is an avid reader of *Poetry Review* and has bookshelves of the stuff, most of which he claims he can't understand. Asked if he considers himself first and foremost a comic or a poet, he immediately defends accessibility, declaring that the most valuable thing is to make people laugh and that the problem with most poetry is that 'it don't make any sense'. Yet he was wounded by Dannie Abse's remark that his work wouldn't last and reading recently at The Blue Nose he obviously relished being able to read not as a 'comic' but as a 'poet'. Trying to find a definition for what it is he does he came up with 'heavy light verse'.

As Robert Frost once said 'there are roughly zones' and perhaps in the end it does not matter whether Hegley wears the label of poet or comic. Certainly his work is not as effective on the page as in performance. Reading his new book *Five Sugars Please* (Methuen, £7.99) I became bored without the pauses, the idiosyncratic, slightly manic body movements that give comic weight to his voice. For only in rare cases is the language alone sufficient to sustain the humour and his attempts at more serious verse, despite the word play, seem thin, as in 'Spring': 'sitting tight/ white/upright and unopened/they are a bit like candles/and they make things look holier/these April flowers of the Magnolia'. Yet maybe the problem is ours more than Hegley's. In a cultural climate that is bent on definitions and labels and where even the obviously literary work of young poets is represented as the 'new rock 'n roll', why should Hegley oblige by fitting neatly into any particular aesthetic pigeonhole? What he does, he does with great skill. He has made the world of dogs, glasses, men's facecloths and garden sheds supremely his own. As he said while we finished our coffee 'You can get to some exotic places from the back garden'. To do that is surely a form of poetry.

Unbuttoning the Lip

By Elizabeth Bartlett

Jackie Kay,
Other Lovers,
Bloodaxe, £5.95,
ISBN 185224 2531

Once more, with feeling – Jackie Kay gives us a second collection which is even more impressive than her first, *The Adoption Papers* (Bloodaxe, 1991) which was widely acclaimed and the text produced on Radio 3. She was born in Scotland in 1961 and has also written widely for stage and television. This last fact is not surprising, as her skills with the spoken word are evident in both books. She may, I suppose, become more famous for her plays and perhaps turn to the novel as a means of expression. Anything is likely, but for the time being we have her poetry which is brave and honest, full of pain and rage, but also a tenderness which is not sentimental, but deeply moving. She is also very funny, as Fleur Adcock points out. It is the sheer vigour of her work in whatever mode that makes for an immediacy and a clarity which gives the reader a feeling of emotional release. The control, of course, is in the crafting of the poems, for this is not the kind of poetry any adjudicator of poetry competitions is familiar with, which is poured out recklessly and swamps the reader like a tidal wave.

There seem to have been similar titles by women poets recently (*The Other House* by Anne Stevenson and *The Other Country* by Carol Ann Duffy). Is this something to do with being the other sex? In the case of Jackie Kay this could also be translated into being the other colour, as the adopted child of white parents. In her chilling poem, 'Compound Fracture' a nurse says to a child screaming for her mother in a casualty ward:

Now Now Now, her voice hailstones

pelting – *You won't be seeing your mother*
unless you button
that fat lip, and worse and worse.

'Her eyes bulging with cruelty', one feels the verbal cruelty of the 'thick lip' in this particular context. The poem ends: 'That sardonic tongue; that regiment cap./ My mother was still in another world, taking sips/ of sweet tea for shock; I ached for her soft lips'. The child realises what the nurse had said 'only by looking/ at her body and her lips'. The compound fracture becomes more than the physical accident and more an emotional trauma one feels, and the three pairs of lips become almost symbolical.

There are several sequences of poems which are all powerful and sustained. The sequence about Bessie Smith, the blues singer, has hidden within it the true rhythm of the blues. In the poem 'In the Pullman', it's as if we, the readers, travel too.

Bessie and I are in her Pullman heading for
Tennessee
Bessie and I are in her Pullman heading for
Tennessee
We got so much heartbreak, we can't divide it
easily.

The title sequence of poems is part of her exploration, rooted in the past or the present, the child, the lover, and finally into a kind of autonomy. 'Out and about, you are so confident/ you're taking short cuts, back alleys/ winding your way past yourself,/ up a narrow cobbled close in the big High Street'. This reads like a kind of personal topography of inner and outer worlds. In a further sequence, 'The Year of the Letter' she writes about the demolition of a library and follows the lives of the borrowers, encompassing the power of the written word. The library becomes a place of discovery, a source of knowledge: 'A hundred books flap their pages like broken wings./ Everywhere there is a sign: TO LET – CLOSING DOWN / The big ball swings again; again'. There is not a duff poem in this collection, but 'Finger', 'Pork Pies', 'Going to See King Lear', 'Watching people Sing' and 'Therapy' were my personal favourites.

In a review of a recent anthology of women's poetry [Patricia Craig on *Sixty Women Poets*, *PR*, Vol 83 No 4], the critic complained of some of the poems making 'a great to-do about deep feelings', chiding women for being 'too wrought-up or too wound-down', and praising only a few established poets, although one of these is ticked off for using a title like 'Night Feed'. When there is a correct balance of craftsmanship and feeling, as in Jackie Kay's marvellous book, we have something so valuable, both to us as readers and to poetry in general that we cannot afford not to read her work and be grateful. It is a pity she is not included in the New Generation Poets promotion which claims to celebrate the rise of the most exciting group of new poets since the Auden generation. Why?

Outsider Trading

by Linda France

Anne Rouse,
Sunset Grill,
Bloodaxe, £5.55, ISBN 1 85224 219 1
Christine McNeill,
Kissing the Night,
Bloodaxe, £5.99, ISBN 1 85225 220 5
Stephen Knight,
Flowering Limbs,
Bloodaxe, £5.95, ISBN 1 85224 246 9
Stephen Smith,
The Fabulous Relatives,
Bloodaxe, £5.95, ISBN 1 85224 213 2

There's something special about the first time for anything and the same goes for first collections, for the poet and for the reader. As a reader, there's always the novelty factor which, if you're lucky, sustains the interest for the duration of the book, the discovery of a new voice, a new version of the world. Perhaps that's what Brodsky meant when he referred to poetry as the 'one night stand' of literature. The best, those that remain in the memory, leave you wanting more, looking forward to seeing what will happen in the next frame.

From the poet's point of view, work contained in a first collection generally spans a very long period, poems appearing in magazines while awaiting publication in book-form. The process continues, informed in the later stages by a new confidence conferred by eventual acceptance. During this long gestation the individual poems accumulate and are ordered as the collection takes on its final unique shape and colour. Or so goes the Platonic ideal.

The thematic pattern that traditionally runs through first collections is predominantly autobiographical, root-tracing. All of these four examples are concerned in one way or another with deracination and dislocation, internal and external. This is 'the poet as outsider', apparently better-placed to observe society's conflicts where they touch upon the poet's own. In a world composed increasingly of outsiders it's not surprising we have so many new poets contributing to the cacophony.

Anne Rouse

Anne Rouse was one of the stars in the firmament of Carol Rumens' *New Women Poets,* and *Sunset Grill* confirms the shine as steely and authentic. In the opening sequence 'A North London Planetary System' she creates her own metropolitan cosmology, assigning to various London characters the qualities of the planets. It is witty and playful, containing all the hallmarks of her style: a taut diction; honed and unexpected language; an askance ironic presentation of twentieth century urban life, coupled with an elegant formality, somewhat in the manner of Auden, a hero at whose feet she drops her final deceptively off-the-cuff 'Memo'.

Rouse was born in Washington D.C. and grew up in Virginia; although she has lived in London since reading History there. Her voice is recognizably American in its street-wise wryness, layered with a cool awareness of what it means to be 'englished'. The poetry is always active and energetic, offering a clearsighted appraisal of petty concerns and larger betrayals, the games that people play following the rules of denial. Certainly bizarre, it would also be slightly absurd if it weren't so truthfully disturbing: 'Outside there is no tenderness at all'.

Seedy characters like Mister and Missus, Mackenzie and Dougie people her poems, leaving their 'rankness', their 'bourn of mist, under 'a handout/of rain'. The careful handling of irony is reflected in the off-setting effect of titles such as 'Dejeuner sur l'Herbe', 'Success', 'Virginian Arcady', 'Athletic' and 'Fortuna'. Although modest, Rouse never sells herself short. There is no doubt about the quiet strength of her voice, despite the back hand from her muse who 'talked low, reproachful, pretty: /Said I don't love her enough'. Her 'Homage to Jean Rhys' invites comparison with that writer's qualities – a sure touch with the rackety underworld, a spare precision and a lyrical elegance; proof, if needed, that words are much more than simply 'bandages'.

Christine McNeill

The work of Christine McNeill also explores her foreign background (this time, Austria) as well as her life in Britain since 1970. In her intense and claustrophobic poems, she recounts stories of her family's experience of the War. She appears to have inherited their guilt and this becomes the source of her personal dislocation. This is played out in her awareness and examination of her mother tongue, a constant reminder of her legacy of an uneasy and disturbing past. Even boiling a kettle and explaining the de-furrer (der Führer) to a German guest, there is no escape from memory. Even as they are tugged out, roots still remain as admissible evidence, above ground.

The poems are fuelled by a perception distorted by difficulty and pain; this is reflected in their strange juxtapositions, disjointed settings and images that convey an emotional tenor while leaving dark unexplored spaces. One of these spaces is structure: there are occasional infelicities of rhythm, line-endings and punctuation. Another is language, at times clumsy and imprecise: 'As a child I thought the crystalline/in the granite eyes'.

The sense of dislocation is carried over into the poems set in England, focusing on the distance between individuals. For McNeill, against the unavoidable backcloth of violence and hatred, everything comes down to 'Mother Mystery', with too few possibilities of intimacy or understanding. Anne Stevenson found these poems 'intriguing'. I found them disconcerting (good) and frustrating (bad) There's too much need here, poems desperate to be written, still in process, too often failing to take on the requirements of the reader and poetry itself, in terms of language and form.

Stephen Knight

Stephen Knight's best writing uses the human body, dysfunctional and dismembered, to carry his vision. The tone is dispassionate, ironic, surreal, conjuring up a world that is fragmented, populated by strange and deficient characters, whose best is never good enough. His poems are built like stage-sets signalling disorientation, as in the limp seaside town in 'Double Writing' where

> Wind sizzles through trees
> while, from the promenade, waves reach for
> the last bus
>
> back into town. Ticking over in the back seat
> somebody sleeps it off. His thumb is in his
> mouth.

His internalization and embodiment of his disaffection for an unsympathetic, unsatisfactory world by using anatomical imagery is extremely successful. The reader is necessarily implicated and can only feel aghast, checking out her own health and wholeness. A father is accused of being embarrassed by poetry; this poetry is certainly playing for a reaction. And it gets it – horror, fascination and admiration; never embarrassment.

What it could be is depressing, were it not so

well-crafted and amusing, in a sick sort of way. Generally, unlike the various body parts endlessly categorized and laundered, the poems, with titles like 'The Reproductive Organs', 'The Eyeball Works', 'The Body-Parts Launderette', 'The Wig Replacement Clinic', are well put together but still surprising. Their strangeness grows into something beautiful, elegant and very, very healthy.

Knight's world is decidedly unsafe; there are monsters who 'queue/behind the valance until dew/curdles on the garden', a stepfather 'pissing on the toilet seat', a sweater that with its 'ten fingernails push through the flesh like roots'. Everyone is ill or becoming so and it is only in dreams 'WE ALL RECEIVE THE LETTERS WE WANT'.

It is the central section, a sequence, 'Notes For a Poem Called Me, Me, Me', that too thoroughly enacts the fragmentation dealt with so skilfully in the body metaphors of the individual poems. It is too disjointed and unprocessed, smacking of self-indulgence. In the end it does remain only 'notes'.

Stephen Smith

What 'flowering limbs' are to Stephen Knight, his 'fabulous relatives' are to Stephen Smith, and the resulting poems, although still charting the world of dislocation and disenchantment, are possibly more vital because of that. They contain after all *whole* people; even though these are, at his own admission, largely the product of Smith's fertile imagination: the truth, distorted by individual perception, memory and language itself, which takes on a powerful life of its own, as 'the sea edits life's coming and going' and 'rain alliterated days on end'.

Smith revels in 'taking liberties with the dead', making a mythology of his family tree as well as his own and others' experience of what reads like a modern Grand Tour – poems set in Japan, Yugoslavia, India, Thailand, England, Scotland and Wales. Even at home, wherever that might be, there is a sense of foreignness, exclusion. The poet is an outsider in a world full of outsiders, butterfly girls and cortina boys, where it's difficult to tell the living from the dead, who 'stand up straight like trees'. This world is an eminently self-conscious one where death is perceived as only another disproven absolute.

He is at his most self-referential, albeit obliquely, in the Hathaway poems at the very end of the collection, where he uses the contrivance of a feckless alter-ego, offered support and succour from 'the good' in which he cannot whole-heartedly believe. However he is essentially a chancer, with luck and his own imagination on his side, helping him to survive by the skin of his teeth.

The poems have a keen sense of rhythm, are formally proficient and able to avoid the superficially tricksy by their genuine tone. Smith is trying to comprehend the incomprehensible and, like Lear's Poor Tom, 'will continue to mince and to fret,/his mad song dispersed in their rage'. Their rage is also his own, his 'attempts to argue with (himself)', entirely appropriate for the world he has chosen to chronicle, where all is fabulous, all is relative.

On Second Name Terms

by Sean O'Brien

Martin Mooney,
Grub,
Blackstaff, £5.95, ISBN 0 85640 500 0
Desmond Graham,
The Lie of Horizons,
Seren, £5.95, ISBN 1 85411 084 5
Angela McSeveney,
Coming out with it,
Polygon, £6.95, ISBN 0 7486 6137 9
Sue Stewart,
Inventing the Fishes,
Anvil, £7.95, ISBN 0 85646 248 9
James Harpur,
A Vision of Comets,
Anvil, £7.95, ISBN 0 85646 257 8

Martin Mooney's *Grub* is a large and ambitious book, combining a collection's worth of individual poems with the title piece, a narrative in twenty-four parts set in a phatasmagoric 1980s London characterized by rum, bum and misdemeanour. The characters and speakers include Grub himself, 'the brains' behind a no-hope band (The City Reptiles) along with his 'friends' Joe Cancer, Sinead and Annie, doomed ingenues of the Irish underclass. Hanging from Blackfriars Bridge or drifting in the wreck of the *Marchioness*, Roberto Calvi adds a commentary on capitalism. Inspector Stubb reflects on the problems of civil order. A Tory MP dies with a candle up his backside. It's a vivid, intriguing piece of work. If it doesn't entirely succeed, this is partly because the interrelations of persons and theme appear willed, and partly be-cause Mooney writes the whole thing as if it's already finished. On the other hand, he has tapped into a realm of possibility which deserves a more extended outing. The parallels with *Bleak House* are interesting, though what the re-runs of meetings with the dead drawn from Heaney, Eliot and before are actually doing apart from adding the store of allusions is not certain.

Mooney's language is largely the urbane vernacular which seems to be the mean average occupied by younger Irish poets. A knowing griminess occasionally arrives at lyricism, but the result is not yet original. There are nods to Muldoon and Paulin, as well as occasional narrative resemblances to Sweeney in the shorter pieces. I enjoyed the book a good deal, especially 'Fleadh', where Kavanagh's lung is kept in a jar in a pub, and the intriguing 'Fishermen'.

Desmond Graham

It's odd that it's taken so long for a full collection of Desmond Graham's work to become available. His poems have been appearing in magazines and anthologies for years. Good for Seren, then, to have recognized his quality. *The Lie of Horizons* opens with poems about the writer's parents, but really hits its stride with a series about England. 'Our Hunting Fathers' catalogues the immense variety of murdered animals displayed about the nation, including butterflies 'nailed to the table top' and moths –

> for them, our hunting fathers strolled to the
> lawn end,
> turned on the light, and waited:
> and all next day for all their love of
> cleanliness,
> right through to the next century
> smelt of gas.

'Mrs Thatcher's England' offers another disturbing list, manifestly about the recently here-and-now but also partaking of the Forties and Fifties, while in 'Snapshots' Leeds, York and Durham get a going-over. Hard to resist quoting the last of these entire:

Even the surrounding landscape
is imported from Hampshire.
The miners are redundant.
The prisoners out of sight.
You hear their souls
in a rattling of car keys
in the cathedral close
followed by a shrill blast
of laughter.

In 'I Dreamt I was in England' the speaker wakes and asks '"how could the people of England / be so evil?" and an English friend said / "We have always been evil" / and I could not agree'. That seems to be his subject, at times very directly and memorably handled.

Angela McSeveney

Angela McSeveney's *Coming out with it* contains a disarming poem called 'Reviewed', in which the reviewer is implicitly compared with a Games Mistress at school (ouch): 'It's the first time since PE/ that I've been called/ just by my surname'. The poem closes, 'In the distance, Mrs Turner bawls/ McSeveney, ran it under a cold tap!' The humour is typical of McSeveney's best work, where power, 'showing off', sex and troublesome individuality are all in play. She can write accurately and with unsettling bluntness, often about standing on the sidelines of an event – the threat of breast cancer, the permanent waiting room of unemployment, a childhood of abrupt changes of address, an erotic life unsuited to the pages of *Cosmopolitan*. It makes a change from all the genteel local history and grave-sniffing by which we are still mysteriously beset.

When I consider the book as a whole I'm less certain about McSeveney's work. Its avoidance of rhetoric, its plainness, and what it's hard to avoid calling its wry understatement, all come to seem a bit unrelieved. How far can these methods carry her? Perhaps the absence of style becomes as evasive as the most studied mannerism. Polygon seem to like long books; maybe they should like editing them, too. But I await McSeveney's next with interest.

Sue Stewart

Sue Stewart's *Inventing the Fishes* has a beautiful cover – a monochrome picture called 'Brown Trout Rising' by Colin Paynton. It's not clear what the medium is (engraving?) but it's an exhilarating and in a sense very English picture. If the poems worked in the same way there'd be celebrations. But they don't, quite, though they seem to aim for a compara-

ble delicacy and exactitude. There are problems from the outset. Here is the opening stanza of the opening poem, 'When':

When you know you must change
you look back at the leaves
like a shadow, inventing reasons
for staying small.

Are the leaves or 'you' like the shadow? In either case, how and to what effect? Are both true? Does it matter? The poem picks up after this with a few more solidly rendered properties, but like a number of others in the book it has the feel of an exercise – seriously conducted, but an exercise. In the sequences 'Book of Hours' and 'Genesis' there are frequent local felicities, but the atmosphere can be a bit precious, and there is a lack of really compelling themes to accompany the privilege accorded to moody settings and strangely decontextualized Nature. John Burnside, a poet to whom Stewart sometimes seems a distant cousin, deals in comparably minute apprehensions, but his work feels driven as Stewart's does not. The aim may be exquisiteness, it's hardly served by constructions like this one, from 'Apple': '

After rain, drips from the roof.
The garden has that rinsed look
and still heavy, skin-soaked
from its shower of wands.

James Harpur

James Harpur's *A Vision of Comets* does even less for me, I'm afraid. It may be that nowadays there is a community of religious poets with its own house rules; otherwise it's hard to account for these lines from 'Tallis: Spem in Alium':

Up the polychromatic sound soars
In sudden intense undulations,
Transporting us to beyond the stars,

Till at last the threads are all drawn tight
Into one glorious unification,
As spectral colours pour into white.

Humility is one thing; but this strenuous banality raises the suspicion that the poet is misunderstanding the relation between language and subject. If Harpur's concern is often with 'the numinous', he has a funny way of turning vision into commentary. The author received a Gregory Award – presumably the sort you can collect at petrol stations.

➤ *News/Comment*

Poetical Chairs

The principal organizations that support poetry are going through one of their periods of reshuffling at the top. Chris Meade arrived as Director of the **Poetry Society** in January from a background in imaginative literary promotion work at Sheffield and Birmingham libraries. Two of his early ideas: to produce an information pack to accompany the New Generation promotion, and to open up the Society's Covent Garden HQ from April as a resource centre selling selected books such as the New Gen titles, *Poetry Review* and *Poetry News*, Poems on the Underground, and to provide on-the-spot advice and information.

At the **Poetry Book Society,** Director Brian Perman saw through the new £5000 T. S. Eliot Prize before moving on to become Director of Book Trust, the Booker and Forward Prize organizers, amongst other things. PBS manager Martha Smart is now Director. The Eliot Prize found a good fresh winner in Ciaran Carson's *First Language*, a remarkable book that should make Carson an automatic inclusion in lists that begin: Heaney, Longley, Muldoon, Mahon, and Paulin. *First Language* will be reviewed in the next *Poetry Review*.

The Arvon Foundation, which had its 25th anniversary in 1993, has a new Chairman. Lawrence Sail has completed a stint of four years in which a third, Scottish, Centre was added and Arvon returned to central Arts Council funding. The new Chairman is Brian Cox, a poet whose *Collected Poems* were published by Carcanet last year, a founding editor of *Critical Quarterly*, and an educationist who chaired the National Curriculum English Working Group in 1989. The 1994 course tutors include several New Generation poets (David Dabydeen, Kathleen Jamie, Michael Donaghy, Simon Armitage, Glyn Maxwell, Don Paterson, Jamie McKendrick) and also Michèle Roberts, Fleur Adcock, Helen Dunmore, Wendy Cope and many more.

The joker in the pack is the **National Centre for Literature, Swansea,** a £3m plus project initiated by Lord Palumbo as part of the Arts 2000 initiative. After the debacle of Maura Dooley's resignation as Director of the UK Year of Literature and Writing 1995 project, based at the yet to be built National Centre, a flurry of press releases suggests that the phoenix is attempting to rise. The building will now be a restored former Guildhall, and plans have been released ('The piazza to the south of the building will be finished sensitively with granite paviors and York Stone pavings and the area will be enclosed with a railed dwarf wall'). Maura Dooley's replacement as Director of the Year of Literature and Writing is Sean Doran, who unlike her has no background in literature. He is a graduate of East Anglia in Music and Fine Art, a newspaper art critic and organiser of the mixed arts Impact 92 Festival in Derry. The project worker under Doran with responsibility for poetry is David Wooley, a former literature development worker and editor of *Westwords*. To put the project in perspective: the cost of the building alone is about double the Arts Council's annual grants to all literature bodies – the Poetry Society is the only such body to receive more than £100,000. The funding for Swansea comes from the EU, Swansea City Council, the Welsh Development Agency, and West Glamorgan County Council. Under Maura Dooley the project had some credibility – her record at the South Bank suggested she might indeed do great things with that kind of money. But now the project seems to be politics 100 per cent: literature zero. A list of objectives includes:

Writers' & Artists' Yearbook 1994

87th Edition

The indispensable reference book for poets, writers and anyone involved in creative work.

660 pages paperback £9.99

A & C BLACK

'To establish Swansea as the literary capital of Wales and the UK (eat your heart out Huddersfield, not to mention Cardiff, where the Welsh Academy is based). The 'Vision Statement' includes such incoherences as 'A "City of Literature" will be established on every street and in every shop in Swansea'. The Centre is due to open in March 1st 1995, although presumably the junketing will start in January. The Vision Thing ends: 'In 1995 your culture will be our celebration and our culture will be your celebration'. Sheer blind panic by the sound of it.

The Poetry Book Society gives you four dis-counted Choice Books a year, plus Recommen-dations, the Bulletin, and other offers. The first books of Simon Armitage, Glyn Maxwell and Don Paterson were all PBS Choices. UK membership is £26. For further information, contact the Po-etry Book Society, 10 Barley Mow Passage, Lon-don W4P 4PH. Tel: 081 994 6477. For Arvon's 1994 programme of course at Totleigh Barton in Devon, Lumb Bank in Yorkshire and Moniack Mhor in Inverness-shire, write to: The Arvon Foundation, Totleigh Barton, Sheepwash, Beaworthy, Devon EX21 5NS. Tel: 0409 23 338.

Our Back Pages

The New Generation has been unfurling in *Poetry Review* over the last seven years or so. Five of the twenty were highlighted in the magazine's three New Poets special issues since 1987: Elizabeth Garrett and Glyn Maxwell in New British Poets (Winter 1987/8), Don Paterson in New Poets '90 (Autumn 1990), Susan Wicks and W. N. Herbert in Jostling at the Sacred Gate (Autumn 1992). These issues also include other poets who have since come to promi-nence – Eva Salzman, Martyn Crucefix, Mimi Khalvati, Gwyneth Lewis, and Sophie Hannah. New Poets '90 also featured Catch Words, the Poetry Society's Autumn '90 tour with Jackie Kay, Simon Armitage, Glyn Maxwell, and Lavinia Greenlaw – a significant event in the pre-history of the New Generation.

Copies of all three issues are still available and can be bought singly, or in a special New Genera-tion offer of three for £9.00 including postage. New British Poets costs £3.00, New Poets '90 £3.50, Jostling at the Sacred Gate, £5.00, all in-cluding post and packing. For a full list of *Poetry Review* back numbers please send an SAE.

Report on No. 27: Po Soc Blues

The New Generation has rejuvenated the Poetry Society. As recently as last September it was riven with strife. We invited poems on the subject.

Vers de Poetry Société

'Heath-Stubbs and I were wondering if perhaps
You'd like to join the Society? Chaps
like you, George, are always welcome.' What for?
I'd find it all a bore.
You know I would. No, nothing could persuade
Me to. And so 'Dear Heath-Stubbs: I'm afraid ...'

Funny how many clubs and things there are.
They meet a human need. But better far,
If you must 'belong', to join Rotary.
Poetry Soc? Not for me.
Besides, with Heath-Stubbs at the helm you'll find
It's a case of the blind leading the blind.

But wait. What's that? There is a magazine?
You should have said. You know I'm always keen
To try and to get my poems into print.
It's possible, you hint.
The mere suggestion is enough to force
A change of heart. 'Dear Heath-Stubbs: Why of
course ...'

George Jowett

I couldn't care less ...

I couldn't care less for the tedious mess
That these posturing poets have got in.
Who cares about motions, and tedious notions
For shoring a building that's rotten.

I read the *Review*, the rest can go stew.
It's poems I'm after, not meetings.
These rows seem to hark back (see *passim* M. Spark)
To ancient dark feuds and unseatings.

Nicholas Murray

No 29: The New Rock 'n Roll

In his Diary (see page 58) Don Paterson sets up the notion of reading poems as if they were rock numbers: 'holding the mike out for the last line as 10,000 adolescents scream "Maxine!" "Laverne!" "Patty!"' (from Michael Donaghy's 'Shibboleth'). Poems on poetry and rock wanted, any angle. Full set of 20 New Generation books to the winner; up to four *Writers' & Artists' Yearbooks* to runners-up. Deadline: July 1st.

Breathing Life into Lowell

Dear Peter,

In my student days, twenty years ago, a professor once directed me to Robert Lowell's *Life Studies*, in order to breathe 'life' into my own writing; well, he certainly woke me up at least. Working backwards and forwards through Lowell's poetry since then has been one of the pleasures of my life.

On a Radio 3 programme in 1984 ('Pity the Planet') Derek Mahon reckoned that, although Lowell's reputation has taken a 'battering' since his death in 1977, 'There seems to be a level beneath which it cannot sink'. That same buoyancy is evident today, in the warm-up to the New Generation Poets promotion. Writing in the *Guardian* in January, James Wood acknowledged Robert Lowell's influence on these young poets ('allowing formal freedoms, personal jottings and the smoky ellipses of the dreamily unsayable'). And yet does this same influence grow from Faber's few, cautious, unannounced reprints that one finds in the larger bookshops?

Where is the *Collected Poems* of Robert Lowell? Where is the critical attention that provides a context for discussion of the poetry? And if a state of 'Lowell neglect' does exists, where is *Poetry Review*?

In 'Dolphin', Robert Lowell famously wrote: 'my eyes have seen what my hand did'. Surely, seventeen years is long enough to keep others from seeing the same? Where is the *Collected Poems*?

Yours sincerely,
Tony Roberts
Manchester
(We hope to print Simon Armitage's Poets on Poets talk on Lowell in a future issue. Ed)